'BEHAVIOURAL ECONOMICS'

RE-SHAPING THE QUALITY OF LIFE

MOHAMED BUHEJI
& DUNYA AHMED

authorHOUSE

AuthorHouse™ UK
1663 Liberty Drive
Bloomington, IN 47403 USA
www.authorhouse.co.uk
Phone: 0800 047 8203 (Domestic TFN)
+44 1908 723714 (International)

© 2020 Mohamed Buheji & Dunya Ahmed. All rights reserved.

No part of this book may be reproduced, stored in a retrieval system, or transmitted by any means without the written permission of the author.

Published by AuthorHouse 01/24/2020

ISBN: 978-1-7283-9806-8 (sc)
ISBN: 978-1-7283-9807-5 (e)

Print information available on the last page.

Any people depicted in stock imagery provided by Getty Images are models, and such images are being used for illustrative purposes only. Certain stock imagery © Getty Images.

This book is printed on acid-free paper.

Because of the dynamic nature of the Internet, any web addresses or links contained in this book may have changed since publication and may no longer be valid. The views expressed in this work are solely those of the author and do not necessarily reflect the views of the publisher, and the publisher hereby disclaims any responsibility for them.

CONTENTS

Introduction vii

Part 1. BE Influence on Quality of Life 1

    Chapter 1 Understanding the Potential of BE on establishing 'Quality of Life' Constructs 3

    Chapter 2 'The Trust Project' Building Better Accessibility to Healthcare Services through BE and Inspiration Labs 33

    Chapter 3 Behavioural Economics Trends in Improving Governments Outcomes – Much more than Nudge 47

    Chapter 4 Re-Inventing Public Services Using Gamification Approaches 74

Part 2. Quality of Life Influence on Future Socio-Economic Life 105

    Chapter 5 Nudge Theory vs. Inspiration Economy Labs- Comparing the Depth of Influence on Socio-Economics Behaviours 107

    Chapter 6 Reviewing Implications of 'BE' on Our Future Life 134

Chapter 7	Practices of Future Foresight in Management of Non-Communicable Diseases : An Early Attempt towards Focusing on 'Foresight Economy' Labs	146
Chapter 8	Gamification Techniques to Re-Invent Public Healthcare Services – A Case Study	167

Conclusion 187
Abbreviations 193
Keywords 195
Who We Are 197
Brief about Editors 199

INTRODUCTION

1.0 Imagine

Imagine there is a new medicine that claims to improve your quality of life (QoL) in one prescription. The medicine is a remedy for all your QoL problems and it is sold at an affordable price. Wouldn't you be excited to buy it? Well, this medicine is available now through more understanding of neuroscience and behavioural economics (BE). It is becoming available and accessible to any community and it does not cost much. You need only to explore it and try it!

2.0 The Current Economy and QoL Gap

Since Ibn Sina era, the link of behavioural techniques and its influence on healthcare and wellness are under investigation and exploration. However, over the years and after the industrial revolution, this horizontal approach thinking was disregarded. The world became more capital-driven mindset and the spread of the vertical thinking emphasised the importance of specialities and sub-speciality over the holistic horizontal thinking. The development of vertical thinking helped in developing lots of bad habits, along with higher preventive and corrective costs. Therefore, this book emphasis throughout its chapter that both BE and IE approach QoL problems in a holistic way.

Since the 1960's there have been scattered efforts that analyse the influence of economy in QoL; however, these efforts never been consistent, nor did they link BE clearly with QoL. In this edited book, we bring collective of published papers that show how behavioural economics (BE) and other relevant concepts and methodologies, as inspiration economy (IE) and gamification; which all work together today as a remedy for improving the different issues that deteriorate our quality of life (QoL). The selected work in this book target to build clear evidence on how BE started to shape more our QoL in a way never been experienced before.

3.0 The Way this Book Work

With all the changes in the world today more attention to QoL is needed, in a non-classical way. Therefore, the chapters investigate how through BE, and relevant methodologies as IE, more return and benefits can overcome the constrains capitalism on the quality of life.

BE explains the problem, or the socio-economic issue from the human behaviour perspective. The solution would be tested by engaging the providers and beneficiaries in a common goal. All these approaches focus on using the principle of 'loss aversion' that show the possibilities of gain vs loss, which can perfectly suites the purpose of motivating all the stakeholders toward a better quality of life decisions.

The book is divided into two parts; the first part focuses on BE Influence on QoL. The first chapter in this part shows the rapid developments in the diagnosis of human behaviour, and behavioural sciences in general, and how they reflected in the economic and socio-economic problem-solving. With the emergence of many studies as a result of the application of the Functional Magnetic Resonance Imaging (fMRI).

The impact of behaviours on humans' decisions and in the achievement of their aspirations have started to reflect on the efforts of improving the communities' quality of life. fMRI and other brain and emotional gadgets now are exciting many economists to pay more attention to optimising the role of thinking, mind, spirit and heart in different industries. This chapter shall explore the future impact expected of behavioural economics on the realised meanings and means of QoL, as per OECD (2017) requirements.

The second chapter bring in the issue of building trust, as a tool for BE and IE, with specific focus on healthcare services. Since many decisions relevant to trust are taken every day in critical community-related organisations, both BE and IE labs could make a significant differentiation in building new pathways that correct the consumers' perceptions about the services and create a significant difference to our life. The chapter addresses how the quality of life of the patients and especially those of 'emergency cases' could be treated at the right time and get their rights in admission.

Chapter three is about BE role in improving governments quality of life outcomes towards the betterment of their societies. The role of specific BE approaches is investigated in relevance to its capability for shaping government services. The main BE approach, Nudge, is compared to IE Labs (IL's), in relevant to their capacity to capture opportunities and in creating a differentiation. Both BE and IE labs create a wave of 'influence without power' towards the community social welfare issues and more specifically QoL. The comparative study in this chapter shows the spirit the success stories bring due to the transformation created by BE.

Chapter four talks about how gamification is still an emerging field in social sciences with a growing interest in its application in public services. Yet, most of the published literature on gamification focus on the utilisation of electronic games and serious games, as a methodology for the development of public services; rather than seeing how to apply gamification approaches in developing these services. Thus, the rationale for this chapter is to develop the capacity of the public sector to re-invent itself through the utilisation of gamification techniques that optimises the use of neurosciences.

The second part of this book focuses on quality of life influences on the future socio-economic life. It starts with chapter five by comparing nudge theory that was mentioned in the first part vs IE labs. The acknowledgement of Noble Prize to the importance of BE as a democratic economy shows the development of behavioural applied economics as an important field in life. The psychology of both nudge and inspiration economies are compared to the mechanism of social engineering.

Chapter six reviews the development of BE and its influence on our life today and its possible implications in the future. The review evaluates how the behavioural theories would create new thinking, especially with the increasing of the repeated financial crisis. The chapter shows the essential BE theories, perspectives, trends and developments along with their implications on our future life.

Chapter seven looks at the future foresight of the technological changes that brings along innovative disruptions rather than only socio-economic challenges. With the development of the foresight of the future, science efforts should be directed towards tackling humanity chronic problems than just focusing most of the efforts on future technological developments and advancements only. Focusing the foresight analysis on the increase of Non-Communicable Diseases (NCD's) does not only help us to tackle current and future health community issues, but also direct the focus of the efforts towards mitigating the progressive development of the future socio-economic and quality of life challenges.

The case study in chapter eight focuses on the interesting gamification techniques that could re-invent public healthcare services. The editors are emphasising that the growth in gamification in the different public services could enhance the development of engagement of the concerned stakeholders with different QoL initiatives. The chapter investigates how the different gamification constructs and techniques could help in re-inventing the public healthcare services.

Finally, we hope this work would excite you as a reader to investigate more the techniques of behavioural economics, inspiration economy and gamification and explore their capacities in creating positive change in our life today and the future.

PART ONE

BE INFLUENCE ON QUALITY OF LIFE

CHAPTER ONE

Understanding the Potential of BE on establishing 'Quality of Life' Constructs[1]

2.1 Introduction

BE has developed very rapidly in the past three decades and has become the leader of all new democratic economies. This interest has increased with the recognition of the Nobel Prize for this behavioural liberal economics, which has given hope to new economies such as the economy of inspiration. In the same time, leading governments have become thinkers and resources that give greater importance to the implementation of BE tools to improve the outcomes of government services towards improving their communities. Therefore, this chapter examines the role of modern BE two main approaches to focus on their role in improving the quality of life, especially in developing countries. The Economist (2012), Buheji and Ahmed (2017a); Sanders and Halpern (2014).

---

[1] Buheji, M. (2018) Understanding the Potential of Behavioural Economics on Establishing 'Quality of Life' Constructs, American Journal of Economics, 8(6): 279-288.

BE is considered one of the most promising coming economies that focuses on exploring the potential forces or the capacity within the intrinsic power of the communities. Among these economies are the economies of knowledge, inspiration, resilience and youth that use the laboratory methodology to see opportunities in a challenge. They are called in general Inspiration Labs. In this study, we will identify the impact of these Labs on the speeding up the achievement of quality of life indicators. Buheji and Ahmed (2018), Thaler (2015).

The chapter presents the results of the new behavioural economics and how researchers and practitioners can benefit from them for future QoL initiatives. The methodology and then discussion shows how these BE approaches are disciplined and ultimately lead to outcomes and impact that improves the quality of lives of communities while developing the human mentality and raising its ability to explore. Nagatsu (2015).

2.2 The Importance of this Study

The theoretical and practical importance of the study is that it builds a rare relationship between the 'quality of life' and the creation of 'BE' practices and exploring the intrinsic capabilities of institutions through focused laboratories. As for practical importance, it clarifies to the scientific and local community the differences between the economics of behaviours of all kinds and ways of applying them to the advancement of society and institutions.

2.3 Literature Review

2.3.1 Introduction to Behavioural Economics

BE combines the fields of psychology, economics, management and changes with sociology to contribute to the development of the communities and solving complex problems, along with making more effective decisions that bring betterment to economics and communities development. This collective science of behavioural economy examines the field of behaviours change which has psychological, social, cognitive and emotional opportunities reflected on the quality of life. BE laboratories have shown to have the role of social engineering in relevance to improving the socio-economic decisions of individuals, institutions, communities and resource revenues (Sunstein, 2015), Buheji (2018b). Therefore, it is not surprising that many scientists have won the Nobel Prize in the past 30 years, such as Richard Thaler (2017), Daniel Kaneman (2002), George Ackeroff (2001), Gary Becker (1992) Simon (1978).

2.3.2 Definition of Quality of Life

QoL can be defined as the practice of upgrading the social, health, psychological and environmental aspects of life to achieve a decent, safe and stable life, for every individual and family in the community. Successful QoL programs are expected to promote patterns of choices for the best life practices by providing more options for citizens, Buheji (2016). OECD (2017) specified that QoL could be represented and measured by the following main constructs: housing, income, jobs, community, education, environment, civic engagement, health, life satisfaction, safety and work-life balance.

Quality of life focuses on improving political, environmental, social and cultural factors that positively affect overall health, such as providing security, renouncing violence, reducing poverty, eliminating unemployment, education, providing healthy housing and protecting the environment. It also focuses on the quality of life of people exposed to risk affecting healthy lifestyles such as smoking. The quality life practices might mean thus enhancing the physical activity, or healthy food, or personal hygiene, or the proper management of health facilities such as emergency rooms or health centres and safety on the road. Buheji and Ahmed (2018), Barcaccia (2013), Johnston et al. (2009).

2.3.3 Improving Quality of Life Indicators – the Bahraini experience

Many countries have done different work relevant to the quality of life, specifically in the last decade. However, few have been related to national plans. Within the framework of a project undertaken by the researcher with the government of the Kingdom of Bahrain; over a period of several years, significant indicators in several fields of the quality of life were measured and identified. The researcher identified with the leaders of the Government of Bahrain the role of government institutions in creating quality of life indicators that influence the behaviour of the citizens and in the same time help to create development towards the country's vision 2030. The QoL indicators were set to improve the aspects of social, health, psychological and environmental life, which would lead to the satisfaction of the individuals and the families besides all the society. These indicators promote patterns of best practices of life through the availability of options for citizens and residents. The efforts of the Inspiration Labs have therefore been concentrated in the following five areas:

First - Family stability - Provide security and stability for the family of various types and social conditions to reach a safe and stable family environment by ensuring the needs of the family and enhancing their health and psychological integrity through family cohesion and self-reliance.

Second- Health Protection - to raise the level of public health of the individual and the practices related to community health promotion and prevention before treatment. As well as protecting the Bahraini society from non-communicable diseases as a shared responsibility among all groups of society through the optimal use of resources to reduce disease, death and disability due to non-communicable diseases and its complications.

Third- Education Outcome- to raise the level of teaching and learning in all its forms.

Four- Economic Development – to raise the economic impact of the citizens and differentiate intrinsic power resources.

Five- Protection of Environment and Natural Resources- To promote the values of sustainable development to preserve human life, and to protect the environment and the natural use of natural resources. As well as protecting, rehabilitating and improving the environment through community partnership.

These five areas contribute to the enhancement of quality of life and the development of infrastructure and services that promote health and environmental health, reduce traffic injuries and reduce transport from harmful emissions. They also contribute to providing the best types of housing services suitable for citizens with low incomes to ensure their stability and achieve decent living conditions. Blanding (2017); Tinkler (2011).

2.3.4 Behavioural Economy and its Approaches

Socio-economic research, policies, practices and processes, with all its traditional tools that emerged almost three centuries ago, proved today that they are insufficient to the development of human achievements. So the behavioural economy came to call on methodologies that connect psychology and economics in many ways.

There are many approaches in BE that depends on ideas of a 'single way of thinking', Nudge is one example. However, in this chapter, we closely focus on the approach of Inspirational Labs which can be characterised by 'different ways of thinking' as it uses exploration techniques for discovering hidden opportunities with visualisation of broader objectives in life. Buheji (2016), Thaler and Sunstein (2008). Sugden (2009) have all reviewed how these BE approaches to develop a simple change in the environment of the targeted community which have a significant impact on the community behaviour and thus in subsequent economic situations. Sugden (2009) justified that these economic approaches can be like small interventions that encourage individuals to make different decisions. The Economist (2012) and Buheji (2018b).

2.3.5 Theory of Nudge and Quality of Life

Nudge theory is the foundation of a concept that contributes to a social and perhaps even a relatively large and hidden socio-economic transformation. It encourages people to make decisions that are in their broad personal interest and the interest of governments to achieve their role towards setting a better standard of living. The theory of Nudge is based on Richard Thaler, and Cass Senstein book which focuses on knowing how people think, and how we can make it easier for them to choose the best for themselves, their families and their community thus makes it easier for these citizens to make certain decisions for the betterment of life. Cambridge (2018); Hansen (2016); Samson (2015), Thaler (2015), Sunstein (2013).

2.3.6 The Impact of Economics of Inspiration on Quality of Life

One of the best contemporary works that focused on the exploration of inspiration and its uses is the study of Thrash and Elliot (2004), where inspiration is defined as a state of transformation into new qualities that ignites a continuous flutter of the soul and contributes to the development of creative ideas that can lead to an effective outcome. This creative outcome comes through tangible creative approaches that influence the type of services delivered in society. Recent studies explore how the approaches of the inspiration currency can affect transformations from being situational to becoming sustainable.

2.3.7 Psychology and Economics

Economic theories are usually based on how people make decisions. However, over the past three decades, there has been significant development of 'positive psychology' and socio-economic behaviour. Inspiration-style laboratories, similar to Nudge methodology, mainly come from the fields of psychology, economics, sociology and change management. Nagatsu (2015)

All studies published in the past 20 years, such as Ariely (2008; Shiller, 2005; Cialdini, 1998), demonstrated the importance of behavioural and psychological factors in the shaping of social, environmental and economic decisions and outcomes. These and other authors argue that social and behavioural factors are important to eliminate the limitations of individual choices and prevent them from building an integrated personality and complete information, or building unregulated cognitive ability or self-control (Sugden, 2009).

Inspiration Labs and their applications have many practices that contribute to the industry of happiness and well-being and build common psychological bridges with other concepts to establish the quality of life practices. Inspiration Labs promote mutual thinking towards a better quality of life for communities because they are linked to exploration endeavours. This type of attempt helps people mitigate the challenges they face in life, overcome failure, break risk aversion, build strong personalities and have a strong ability to learn and adapt.

2.3.8 BE Applications in Quality of Life

BE applications in quality of life acts as an alert, and opens up more options. For example, in the UK, Nudge was used in improving public services, and managing pensions. (Instituteforgovernment.org.uk.2010). Government departments in Denmark, Australia, Canada and the Netherlands have also launched similar programs in health care, such as obesity treatment, social welfare such as unemployment compensation, energy efficiency, household recycling and consumer credit. Wilkinson (2013)

McAuley (2007) and Samson (2015) explored the use of design engineering and options which contributed to solving many social problems and reducing their negative impact. While Thaler and Sunstien (2008) study found to selectively structure contributions to predictably changing people's behaviour without significantly preventing any options or changing their economic incentives. For example, this guided choice makes it easier to avoid unhealthy food in the cafeteria, or join the plan to raise the contribution to the pension fund.

As for the inspiration labs which were established in the government program in the Kingdom of Bahrain and led by researcher and continued for three years. The impact of inspiration engineering and its laboratories on the use of hidden problems and opportunities of quality of life touched many areas as basic and higher education, social development, electricity and water services, primary care, secondary care, public health, psychiatric services, applied sciences, industry, commerce, training and development, social security fund, quality assurance in education, labour market and fund, women's council, customs, visas, passports services, municipal services, the national centre for exhibitions and conferences, road works, the tender board, housing services, police and security services, ports, maritime services and land ownership and registration. (Buheji and Ahmed, 2016; Buheji, 2015).

2.3.9 Influence Without Authority and Quality of Life Requirements

In order to create a positive change in any culture, people need to feel that they had the choice of choosing their paths in relevant to the quality of life decisions. To 'influence without authority' or 'influence with minimal resources; means we need to deal with chronic social and economic problems such as poverty, low ambition to achieve a role in life, low quality of life, low youth productivity, social and political instability, low productivity, high youth migration and business instability issues; using intrinsic powers, Buheji (2018c). As mentioned in Buheji (2016 and 2018a), power-free methodologies contribute to increased demand for more waves of innovation, co-existence, and flexibility, which can lead to more significant results for communities (Cohen and Bradford, 2005). Therefore, this chapter would investigate and focus on inspiration labs more than Nudge as a representative for BE where the approach would be tested for its type, rather than level of influence in creating a better quality of life.

2.4 Research Methodology

A qualitative methodology is used through tables that target to illustrate the differentiated impact of two methodologies of BE and their benefit in creating the quality of life indicators that were set by OECD (2017). Hence, the target is to compare the benefits of both Nudge and Inspiration Labs on the field of Quality of Life Industry based on the proven history of differentiation and the value-added characteristics of both approaches. The research aims to clarify the level of 'return of behavioural change' that has been created, the level of 'capacity development' and the 'impact on social welfare' beside the 'change of mindset'.

Twenty-five types of business sectors which have a direct impact on the communities' life were selected for measuring the influence of the two BE approaches in order to ensure on what areas did it influence in QoL taking again OECD (2017) QoL framework as a reference. The following are the businesses identified:

1. Education
2. High Education
3. Social Development
4. Electricity Services
5. Primary Care
6. Secondary Care (Hospitals)
7. Public Health
8. Health Enrichment
9. Psychiatric Services
10. Pension Fund & Social Insurance
11. Woman Council
12. Municipality Services
13. Labour Market
14. Minimising Traffic Accidents
15. Sewage Sanitary System
16. Municipalities and Urban Development

17. Housing Services
18. Police Services
19. Humanitarian Services Agency (NGO's)
20. Socio-Economic Role of School Dormitory
21. Women Entrepreneurship NGO
22. Graduating and Unemployed Graduate Students Mindset Management
23. Inter-Generations Gap
24. Management of NGO's role in creating better Socio-Economies
25. Improve learning capacities to lifelong learning citizens on activities

2.5 Findings

2.5.1 Basis of Findings

In this study, we mentioned the two main approaches of BE and their level of contribution to QoL. The first method was through research and verification of what is published in scientific research on both approaches. Then the second method was through comparing the outcome of these approaches in relevance to the OECD (2017) framework. This comparison is based on the following key criteria:

A) the level and type of 'behavioural change' that leads to establishing 'quality of life',
B) the level of capacity development achieved through the pursuit of 'quality of life',
C) impact on 'social welfare',
D) 'Change mentality.'

Based on previous criteria, the comparisons focused on ways of dealing with development and behavioural change, the simplicity of the solutions taken and their impact on the level of complexity of the problem, the role in effective decision-making, the method of mentality that contributed to dealing with hidden opportunities and ways of influencing quality of life without extra resources or authority. Buheji (2018b).

2.5.2 Measuring the Impact of Economics of Behaviour and Inspiration on QoL

Based on the synthesis of literature about how to create an impact on QoL outcome in any country or community, one could conclude that focused involvement is needed on specific QoL activities to create a measurable result (Mathieu et al., 2000; Hogg and Cooper, 2007). QoL indicators to be realised in any society need more deep and dedicated work of BE approaches, as the outcome of these approaches found to influence people lifestyle.

In Table (1), we show examples of the work delivered by inspiration labs approach, in relevance to the OECD (2017). The outcome of QoL constructs influenced is gauged in: education, health, safety, civic engagement, community development which enhance the life satisfaction and raise the capacity of more QoL trends, as listed in the table examples. (Buheji and Ahmed, 2017, Dolan et al. 2010).

Table (1) Shows the focus of Inspiration Labs in creating QoL constructs.

Type of Business	Summary of Socio-Economic Type of Inspiring Projects/Models	Quality of Life Constructs
1. Education	1- Inspiring MOE to see the intrinsic powers of Discovering the type of inspired students that can be even better than gifted, competitive and innovative students.	Education Community Civic- Engagement Life-Satisfaction

Type of Business	Summary of Socio-Economic Type of Inspiring Projects/Models	Quality of Life Constructs
	2- Developing creative thinking programs. 3- Discovering Inspiring Students in the right time during their 12 years in education. (Early inspiration discovery program). 4- Establishing track of the inspired students after graduation (Inspiration Pathways). 5- Establishing Inspiration Curriculum and program for its way of delivery through (extra-curricular programs). 6- Establishing Building Inspiration resources 7- Seeing the track of the inspired after graduation. 8- Establishing early inspiration discovery program. 9- Building Inspiration resources within School and after School. 10- Setting Inspired Student Tracking Pathways. 11- Establishing Future Boundary-less Schools 12- Establishing Self-Sufficiency Programs for Schools 13- Re-Inventing the influence of Students Volunteering Programs, including Scouts from Services to measured results and outcomes.	
2. High Education	1- Build a knowledge economy driven practices, including implementation of Lifelong learning skills programs 2- Improve the academic counselling that enhance the students' graduation time and give proper guidance at the right time.	Education Income Community Civic-Engagement Life-Satisfaction

Type of Business	Summary of Socio-Economic Type of Inspiring Projects/Models	Quality of Life Constructs
	3- Improve the University capability to attract competitive projects and contracts through re-organising its knowledge expertise and profile. 4- Establish better readiness for students lifelong learning skills as per the type of speciality and disciplines. 5- Enhance students' fitness or competence to meet labour market demand by encouraging different jobs engagement before graduation. 6- Ensure students finish the requirements of the curriculum in the planned time: i.e., within four years for Bachelor programmes, and one and half years for Masters programmes. 7- Apply Pull-thinking technique to improve academic advisory services. 8- Apply 'smart registration practices' that enhances the students' choices and eliminate waste in opening extra sessions. 9- Optimise Citation for the Country and University through Establishing International Journals. 10- Improving the Return on Investment on every University Centre or College or Accreditation Program. 11- 12- Improve the utilisation paper and the need to print in University Processes. 13- Re-Engineer the integrity of the University Social Responsibility and Industries relation 14- Encouraging Student Contribution to the Socio-economy before graduaion.	

Type of Business	Summary of Socio-Economic Type of Inspiring Projects/Models	Quality of Life Constructs
	15- Ensuring Lifelong Learners Students through an inspiring way of flipped class teaching and ensuring proper preparedness for coming life challenges.	
3. Social Development	1- Improving the Quality of Life of the Elderly/ Geriatric Care Homes through exploring social asset of Day-Care Homes, instead of permanent residency homes. 2- Inspiring the capacity of the productive family program to be more self-independent and attractive for more family members to join as full-time employees/ owners. 3- Building stronger family businesses that have higher Return on Capital Employed (ROCE). 4- Enhance the return from Elderly homecare production 5- Enhance the quality of life of the Disabled People and their Production 6- Easing the process of home care 7- Supporting 'Working from Home' Program 8- Revaluating the Capability of Social Allowance Value and Entitlement – in relevance to Quality of Life with priorities. 9- Enhancing the quality and competitiveness of the product of the Retired & the Disabled 10- Improving the Quality of Micro-Start Families with a focus on Women and People Vulnerability. 11- Improving Quality of Life of Families in isolated communities and tribes (enhance the productivity factors for women and families working from home), with a target to reduce the impact of poverty through eco-tourism projects.	Income Jobs Community Civic-Engagement Health Life-Satisfaction

Type of Business	Summary of Socio-Economic Type of Inspiring Projects/Models	Quality of Life Constructs
	12- Evaluating basis for Poverty Line 13- Transforming care services from the Public Sector to Civic NGOs	
4. Electricity Services	1- Improving the speed at which electricity is connected (9 times) faster. 2- Enhance energy conservation practices by re-engineering the billing scheme and design 3- Improving 'uptime' of electricity supply to 97% to 99% by focusing on scheduling demand response and electricity shedding of through collaborative heavy load consumers' programs. 4- Minimising blackouts or electricity interruptions during hot summers in countries where temperature reach (above 45C) by enhancing sub-stations maintenance programs in collaboration with contractors. 5- Applying more discount for fewer consumption consumers, or the fewer polluters, instead of charging more for more consumption consumers only. 6- Closing the bad debt from the consumers through new attractive payments deals. 7- Collection of utility bills, succeeding in reducing the unpaid government and non-government bills by more than 50% in only three years.	Housing Environment Life-Satisfaction Safety

'Behavioural Economics'

Type of Business	Summary of Socio-Economic Type of Inspiring Projects/Models	Quality of Life Constructs
5. Primary Care	1- Early detection of Non-Communicable Diseases (NCD's), i.e. Diabetes, Blood Pressure, Cholesterol and Obesity. 2- Enhancement of Quality through Inspiring Families Physicians. -Enhancing Triage to patients' priority system in all health centres. 3- Early detection of Psycho-Sematic in relevance to Anxiety in Health Centre. 4- Appointment system for Healthcare. 5- Increase the Health centres readiness for Emergency Cases. 6- Optimising the role of Social Workers and Health Educational Specialist and Health visitors in family screening. 7- Enhancing patients time spent with physicians as per NCDs Risk Matrix. 8- Stream-mapping healthy practices in Educational Institutions towards 'NCD free Generations'. 9- Developing Ideal Family Profile Competition between Health Centres. 10- More Effective Elderly Care Home Visits and management of pre-admission and post-discharge	Community Civic- Engagement Health Safety
6. Secondary Care (Hospitals)	1- Improving the total throughput in Accident & Emergency and speed of admissions through focusing on bed turnover ratio in most congested Hospital Wards (as medical wards) and setting discharge and priority for beds based on Urgency of the cases.	Health Life-Satisfaction Safety

Type of Business	Summary of Socio-Economic Type of Inspiring Projects/Models	Quality of Life Constructs
	2- Enhancing the availability of the Capacity of Beds Utilisation by inspiring towards higher discharges on time and based on defined protocols & follow-up services 3- Reduce Antibiotics use in the main referral hospital 4- Emphasising Peers Review Practice for Complex Cases 5- Finding alternatives for Geriatric Admissions or Geriatric Services within the Hospitals 6- Reducing Radiation to Non-Radiology Medical Staff and patients. 7- Improving essential drugs are available in the central pharmacy, year-round.	
7. Public Health	1- Inspiration in establishing 'Intelligent Inspection' that minimise the rate of poisonous calls or low hygiene fines by 90% with fewer manpower resources & trustworthiness enhancement. 2- Enhancement of the reputation of fast food services that supports local tourism. 3- Intelligent inspection based on pull thinking and lean management that enhanced the outcome of hospitality services and with minimal resources.	Health Housing Community Civic Engagement Life-Satisfaction Safety
8. Health Enrichment	Enhancement of 'Quality of Life' practices & style in coordination with Health Centres	Health Education Life-Satisfaction Safety Work-Life-Balance

'Behavioural Economics'

Type of Business	Summary of Socio-Economic Type of Inspiring Projects/Models	Quality of Life Constructs
9. Psychiatric Services	1- Inspiration of capacity to manage the anxiety to avoid reaching the level of chronic anxiety 2- Reduce the need to treat anxiety with medicines. 3- Reduce suicide ratio due to early treatment of main causalities among youth. 4- Reduce the patients' sick leave due to self-assessments of psycho-sematic symptoms 5- Collaborating with NGOs in early detecting need for psychiatric services	Health Community Education Civic-Engagement Life-Satisfaction Safety Work-Life-Balance
10. Pension Fund & Social Insurance	1- Creating selective thinking in the way of investment of pension fund that would enhance the productivity of the national economy 2- Inspiring the social responsibility plans to ensure that particular type of lower pension jobs is more prepared for entrepreneurship after retirement. 3- Inspiring investment towards enhancement Local Market Stability	Income Jobs Community Health Life-Satisfaction Safety
11. Woman Council	1- Setup an overall outcome and legacy drove national plan that changes the way woman are empowered in Bahrain through giving her more accountability to create social cohesion, stability and national competitiveness. 2- Closing the gap and accelerating the transformation towards 'Women Development' instead of 'Women Empowerment' after five years from the National Plan Kick-off.	Income Jobs Community Health Civic-Engagement Life-Satisfaction Safety

Type of Business	Summary of Socio-Economic Type of Inspiring Projects/Models	Quality of Life Constructs
	3- Ensure knowledge sharing between Business Women, Women Entrepreneurs and Women of Productive Families Programs and especially those of the same or relevant business and link it to gamification rating. (i.e. Rating of Entrepreneurs who contribute and share knowledge)	
12. Municipality Services	1- Building a comprehensive model that proves the local community are ready for effectively segregating and recycling of waste. 2- Showing the role of Municipality in 'Lifelong learning' and 'Qualities of Life' programs through inspiring projects that bridge between (Schools, Families, Local Super Markets, NGO's). 3- Enhancing proactive practices of private companies and NGO's toward Social Responsibility. 4- Speeding up different Municipalities Permits and reducing the need for pre-inspection to 80%.	Housing Civic-Engagement Health Life-Satisfaction Safety
13. Labour Market	1- Shifting Unemployment through inspiring the stratification of Human Capital data and building models in specific industries as per countries sustainable socio-economy needs 2- Minimising unemployment rate through effective counselling 3- Raising opportunities for employment through sourcing type of job opportunities, especially in less demanding jobs 4- Improving locals' employment and demand in areas of hospitality, engineering and nursing 5- Minimise the gap between locals and expat in the main jobs of market demand by defining areas that the national labour should compete.	Income Jobs Work-Life-Balance

Type of Business	Summary of Socio-Economic Type of Inspiring Projects/Models	Quality of Life Constructs
14. Minimising Traffic Accidents	Inspiring traffic accidents reduction efforts through: 1- Enhancing the design towards worst cases, not best cases 2- Improve the speed of repair and active learning on the black spots areas.	Community Safety
15. Sewage Sanitary System	1- Enhancing sewage - drainage system designs 2- Minimise repeated blockages in the sanitary system causes by is station pumps designs. 3- Align the excavation work with water and electricity authority 4- Evaluating Contractors on their performance in managing to build and maintain pumps without blockages. 5- Improve consumers' habits and practices in dealing with sewage system and what goes into the drainage system vs what goes on waste separators. 6- Preventing solid waste or debris from going into the sewage system. 7- Setting transparent program than enhances the awareness about sewage water system utilisation.	Housing Community Health Safety
16. Municipalities and Urban Development	1- Redesigning the public buildings for schools, hospitals to create more multi-purpose buildings owned by the Government and measured for its rate of occupancy and utilisation. 2- Enhance recycling culture and practices, besides prove its financial benefits for decision-makers, without increasing resources. 3- Improve Building maintenance facilities in the early stages of government-owned building designs.	Community Safety Work-Life-Balance

Type of Business	Summary of Socio-Economic Type of Inspiring Projects/Models	Quality of Life Constructs
17. Housing Services	1- Reduce the gap between citizens' demands and their quality of life needs 2- Improving the choices and variety of options in non-villa packages (i.e. flats) 3- Reduce the negative social inequality and improve social coexistence through post-housing services	Housing Community Life-Satisfaction
18. Police Services	1- Reduction of drugs trafficking through refinement and codification of smuggling through reclassification of information. 2- Ease of flow from main points of entry at both airport and ports without an increase in resources or negligence of safety and security + Improving airport immigration officers' services (restore competitiveness spirit). 3- Reduction of gold and jewellery theft from gold market shops 4- Enhance social harmony between neighbours due to parking or similar small issues 5- Reduction courts and legal cases transferred due to family and marriage disagreements by solving it at first instance in the police station. 6- Improving the outcome of creating "Self-Dependent" youth in the 'Police Youth Summer Camps' which is held for three weeks. 7- Reducing police turnover ratio in leaving specific critical units as guarding or working for jail rehabilitation units due to severe and psychologically stress jobs.	Safety Community Life-Satisfaction

Type of Business	Summary of Socio-Economic Type of Inspiring Projects/Models	Quality of Life Constructs
	8- Enhancing maintenance of Police Experts through active 'Experts Appreciation Program' that integrates with Projects Closures. 9- Enhancing Community-based Prevention Policing through improved screening and security assessment (in police stations). 10- Strengthening the social role of the police (the relationship between police stations and community centres). 11- Raising learning and knowledge management in (Economic Crimes). 12- Increasing the efficiency of the performance of senior leaders through prioritization of incoming mail (in Criminal Investigation). 13- Increase the efficiency of patrols (abandoned houses) 14- Raising efficiency and readiness (cadres guard) 15- Enhancing community prevention through improved screening and security assessment (theft of gold shops). 16- Reducing the criminal risk resulting from unregularly employed expats. 17- Enhancing social security by promoting prevention in social tranquillity. 18- Raise confidence through enhanced quality (traffic service). 19- Improve the follow-up service of the communication with the stakeholder in police stations. 20- Rasing Safety Readiness and Evacuation of residential and commercial buildings (Civil Defence).	

Type of Business	Summary of Socio-Economic Type of Inspiring Projects/Models	Quality of Life Constructs
	21- Raising efficiency in gathering inferences in the security centres in order to reduce court rejection or persecutor returning the cases due to insufficient evidence.	
19. Humanitarian Services Agency (NGO's)	1- Reversing the model of poverty support, by making poverty as a temporary condition that we need to prepare the beneficiaries to beyond this stage. 2- Diverting the type of services to be more for sustained income, instead of non-sustainable support 3- Mapping partnership collaboration services (Academic, youth, NGO's, Government, etc.) -Building Cost and Profit centre	Civic- Engagement Income Jobs Health Life-Satisfaction Safety
20. Socio-Economic Role of School Dormitory	1- Showing the benefit and the differentiation of the 'Non-Performing Students' towards the Society and the Socio-Economy. 2- Establishing Students micro start companies 3- Establishing model for dealing non-performing students 4- Showing the self-independence of Religious Studies schools and students (by developing more profit rather than cost centre).	Education Income Jobs Civic-Engagement Life-Satisfaction
21. Women Entrepreneurship NGO	1- Analysing the impact of programs on 'woman development', not only 'women-empower', and the 'living standards' that comes with the 'Quality of Life' in the NGO area and scope of delivery. 2- Optimising the inter-disciplinary learning approach. 3- Enhancing the 'learning by doing' practices 4- Measure the differentiation of women on the economy.	Income Civic- Engagement Life-Satisfaction Work-Life-Balance

Type of Business	Summary of Socio-Economic Type of Inspiring Projects/Models	Quality of Life Constructs
22. Graduating and Unemployed Graduate Students Mindset Management	1- Understanding Dynamics of Labour Market 2- Setting life purposefulness Mindset 3- Challenging transformation towards self- independence and 'Big Picture' Legacy Model 4- Enhancing Employer engagement with schools, colleges and universities and improve the feedback Students interaction and readiness to challenges of the local economy.	Income Jobs Life-Satisfaction Safety
23. Inter-Generations Gap	1- Creating Discussion Group between the different last three generations that identifies: the important difference, the gaps and positivity of intergeneration gap. 2- Setting projects for mitigation of the gaps	Education Civic-Engagement Life-Satisfaction Work-Life-Balance
24. Management of NGO's role in creating better Socio-Economies	1- Creating Discussion Group between the different last three generations that identifies: the respected difference, the gaps and positivity of intergeneration gap. 2- Setting projects for mitigation of the gaps	Community Civic-Engagement Life-Satisfaction Work-Life-Balance
25. Improve learning capacities to lifelong learning citizens on activities	1- Show influence of Disruptive Education and Multi-discipline on creating more inspiring students 2- Simulation experiments & hands-on to enhance community innovation around the university campus.	Income Jobs Education Community

2.6 Discussion

Reviewing all the OoL constructs in Table (1) shows that inspiration labs, as a BE approach, can have a direct influence on OECD (2017) QoL indicators. From the literature reviewed both, Nudge and Inspiration labs seem to focus on the practical application of QoL constructs. However, the integrated approach of Inspiration Labs seems to differentiate its influence on QoL through the models or the projects done in the different fifty businesses listed.

The different projects listed in Table (1) shows that particular BE, IE projects or models there have more impact which addresses more QoL indicators recommended by OECD (2017). The table shows that inspiration labs and similar BE approaches can help in improving the capacity of the communities towards establishing QoL sources such as establishing an effective welfare system with profound changes.

2.7 Conclusion

This chapter identifies the role of modern BE, specifically inspiration labs, in bringing about effective societal change in relevance to QoL. The importance of this chapter is that it fills a gap in the literature in relevance to speeding up the development of the societies quality of life. The chapter sets a clear approach for establishing the quality of life and social welfare. The chapter shows a clear approach for creating a change in the community mindset and the QoL long-term outcomes. The researcher recommends continuing in this line research, because of the wealth of data that could contribute to the developing socio-economies.

Therefore, it is highly recommended to use the opportunities that inspiration labs bring to various governmental and community

QoL issues. More research is recommended in relevance to keeping QoL constructs towards creating new cultures that can bring a variety of solutions to problems and could raise at the same time the quality of life and ineffective ways.

Reference

1. Ariely, D. (2008) Predictably Irrational: The Hidden Forces that Shape Our Decisions. London: Harper Collins.
2. Barcaccia, B. (2013) Quality Of Life: Everyone Wants It, But What Is It? Forbes Education.
3. Blanding, M (2017) Why Government 'Nudges' Motivate Good Citizen Behaviour, HBR https://hbswk.hbs.edu/item/why-government-nudges-motivate-good-behavior-by-citizens, Accessed on: 1/1/2018
4. Buheji, M (2018a) Re-Inventing our Lives, Handbook of Socio-Economic Problem-Solving, AuthorHouse, UK.
5. Buheji, M (2018b) Nudge Theory vs Inspiration Economy Labs- Comparing the Depth of Influence on Socio-Economics Behaviours, American Journal of Economics; Vol. 8, No.3: 146-154.
6. Buheji, M (2018c) "Influencing without Power" Currency in Inspiration Labs—A Case Study of Hospital Emergency Beds. American Journal of Industrial and Business Management, Vol. 8, pp. 207-220.
7. Buheji, M and Ahmed, D (2018a) Exploring Inspiration Economy, AuthorHouse, UK.
8. Buheji, M and Ahmed, D (2018b) Book Review - Handbook of Research on Economic and Social Well-Being, International Journal of Inspiration & Resilience Economy 2018, 2(2): 41-41

9. Buheji, M (2017) Understanding Problem Solving in Inspiration Labs, American Journal of Industrial and Business Management, 7, pp. 771-784.
10. Buheji, M (2016) Inspiring Governments. LAP LAMBERT Academic Publishing.
11. Buheji, M and Ahmed, D (2017a) Breaking the Shield- Introduction to Inspiration Engineering: Philosophy, Practices and Success Stories, Archway Publishing,
12. Buheji, M and Ahmed, D (2017b) Understanding the Role of 'Inspiration Productivity', International Journal of Current Advanced Research Volume 6; Issue 3; April 2017; Page No. 2866-2871.
13. Cambridge Dictionary (2018) Meaning of Nudge, https://dictionary.cambridge.org/dictionary/english/nudge, Accessed on: 10/10/2018.
14. Chetty, R (2015) Behavioral Economics and Public Policy - A Pragmatic Perspective, American Economic Review, American Economic Association, vol. 105(5), pages 1-33, May.
15. Cohen, A., and Bradford, D. (2005) Influence Without Authority (2nd ed.). NJ, Wiley.
16. Dolan, P; Hallsworth, M; Halpern, D and King, D (2010) MINDSPACE Influencing behaviour through public policy, Institute for Government, Cabinet Office. https://www.instituteforgovernment.org.uk/sites/default/files/publications/MINDSPACE.pdf, Accessed on: 10/10/2018
17. Hansen, P. (2016) The Definition of Nudge and Libertarian Paternalism: Does the Hand Fit the Glove? European Journal of Risk Regulation, 7(01), pp.18-20.
18. Instituteforgovernment.org.uk. (2010) MINDSPACE: Influencing behaviour through public policy. https://www.instituteforgovernment.org.uk/sites/default/files/publications/MINDSPACE.pdf, Accessed: 12/4/2018.

19. Jahrami, H and Buheji, M (2012) Reporting a Success Story in the Context of Public Sector: Factors That Matters, Journal of Public Administration and Governance, Vol (2):3, pp. 96-103
http://www.macrothink.org/journal/index.php/jpag/article/view/2470 Accessed on: Accessed on: 10/10/2018.
20. Johnston, R; Pratt, G; Watts, M (2009). Quality of Life, Dictionary of Human Geography (5th ed.). Oxford: Wiley-Blackwell.
21. Kahneman, D (2011) Thinking Fast and Slow, FSG
22. Keating, J (2013) The Nudgy State. How five governments are using BE to encourage citizens to do right thing.
https://www.instituteforgovernment.org.uk/sites/default/files/publications/MINDSPACE.pdf, Accessed on: 10/10/2018.
23. McAuley, I (2007) BE and Public Policy: Some Insights, Working Paper
http://www.home.netspeed.com.au/mcau/academic/bepubpol.pdf, Accessed on: 10/10/2018.
24. Nagatsu, M (2015) Social Nudges: Their Mechanisms and Justification, Review of Philosophy and Psychology, 6 (3), 481-494.
25. OECD (2017) OECD Multilingual Summaries - How's Life? Measuring Well-being
26. Samson, A (2015) The BE Guide, http://www.behavioraleconomics.com, Accessed on: 10/10/2018.
27. Sanders, M., and Halpern, D (2014) Nudge unit: our quiet revolution is putting evidence at heart of government. The Guardian. http://www.theguardian.com/public-leaders-network/small-businessblog/2014/feb/03/nudge-unit-quiet-revolution-evidence, Accessed: 12/4/2018.

28. Sugden, R (2009) On Nudging: A Review of Nudge: Improving Decisions About Health, Wealth and Happiness by Richard H. Thaler and Cass R. Sunstein, International Journal of the Economics of Business, Vol 16, Issue 3, Oct, pp 365-373. https://doi.org/10.1080/13571510903227064, Accessed: 12/4/2018.
29. Sugden, R (2008) Why incoherent preferences do not justify paternalism. Constitutional Political Economy, 19(3), pp.226-248.
30. Sunstein, C (2013) Simpler: The Future of Government, Simon & Schuster.
31. Sunstein, C (2014) Why Nudge? The Politics of Libertarian Paternalism, Yale University Press.
32. Thaler, R (2015) Misbehaving, The Making of BE.
33. Thaler, R and Sunstein, C (2008) The Nudge, Improving Decisions About Health, Wealth and Happiness, Yale University Press.
34. Tinkler, J. (2011) Designing for nudge effects: how behaviour management can ease public sector problems.
35. The Economist (2012) Nudge Nudge, Think Think. The BE use in public policy shows promise, March http://www.economist.com/node/21551032, Accessed: 12/4/2018.
36. Wilkinson, T (2013) Nudging and manipulation. Political Studies 61(2): 341–355, https://www.linkedin.com/pulse/20141102132316-72002586-what-is-nudging-and-some-real-world-applications-of-nudging/, Accessed: 12/4/2018.

CHAPTER TWO

'The Trust Project' Building Better Accessibility to Healthcare Services through BE and Inspiration Labs[2]

4.1 Introduction

Latest behavioural economy studies show that field-tested, small changes in the beneficiaries' environment can have a significant influence on their behaviour and thus can impact the socio-economic situation. Such small interventions can encourage individuals to make different decisions. (Wilkinson, 2013; Ariely, 2008)

Ariely (2008) seen that there are hidden forces that shape our decisions and that rationality plays a good deal of that. As we live in an era where many improvements and progress have

---

[2] Buheji, M (2019) 'The Trust Project' Building better accessibility to Healthcare Services through Behavioural Economics and Inspiration Labs, International Journal of Economics, Commerce and Management, United Kingdom, 7(2): 526-535.

been made on the way that people behaviour is analysed. Dealing with long-term problems as building trust between health centres and patients requires navigating the hidden intrinsic features and that what inspiration labs focus on. The idea of the labs is to test perceptions in the field, and thus the problem exploration journey in inspiration labs would need to be explained.

With the advancement of behavioural economy and IE one would expect more social applications to spread; one of which the 'Trust' based projects. In this study, we shall explore the influence of nudging, the inspiration labs problem solving on building trust on patients for managing the self-prioritisation scheme.

In this chapter, we shall explore 'The Trust Project' that managed to build higher accessibility to healthcare services in primary care centres in the Kingdome of Bahrain. The chapter empirically illustrates how the project in the participating health-centres in Bahrain drastically helped to reduce the morbidity and mortality cases in the health-centres. The project thus shifted the responsibility for defining the urgency of the case from being only the responsibility of the medical staff to being the responsibility also of the patients, by making the patients opting to choose they are mostly non-emergency 'green' case.

4.2 Literature Review

4.2.1 Understanding Behavioural Economy

BE incorporates the study of psychology into economic outcome (Sunstein, 2015). Over the past few decades, there have been many improvements made on the way that people behaviour is analysed. (Hansen, 2016). The concept Nudge, for example, which represent one of the leading tools of the behavioural economy depends focused on knowing how people think, i.e. through field exploration and then designing a procedure or a process that would make it easier for them to choose what is best for them. Thaler and Sunstein (2008) and Sugden (2009).

4.2.2 Defining IE Labs and How they work

IE that focuses on raising the capacity of discovering the potential of human beings' abilities to be the currency of competition and source of a planned outcome and legacy.

Inspiration Labs works on experiential learning psychology and on creating a cognitive process of reflection through a test and then performing observation as part of the exploration of the problem, in our case the problem is the perception of patients self-prioritising for reaching out the family physician in the health centre. The inspiration labs analyse the thoughts and feelings of the concerned stakeholders during the problem-solving process. Such analysis helps us to reveal the 'hidden opportunities' which influence the behaviour development of the patients. Buheji (2016) and Levitt and List (2009).

Dealing with long-term problems requires navigating its intrinsic hidden features and that what inspiration labs focus on. The idea of the labs is to test perceptions in the field and thus pushes us to start to interact with the problem by taking notes and observations to explore the opportunities inside it and in this case, making a pilot of how patients would code themselves. The uniqueness of the inspiration labs is that it engages the stakeholders, i.e. the medical staff in the health centre and to be resilient to manage the problem complexity. Once the opportunities of the problem are identified through the pilot study, we can start realising the potential outcome for the problem and its type of requirement. This is called problem absorption stage. Figure (1) represents the way the problem is realised through inspiration labs. Levitt and List (2009).

Figure (1) Illustration Problem Exploration Journey in Inspiration Labs.

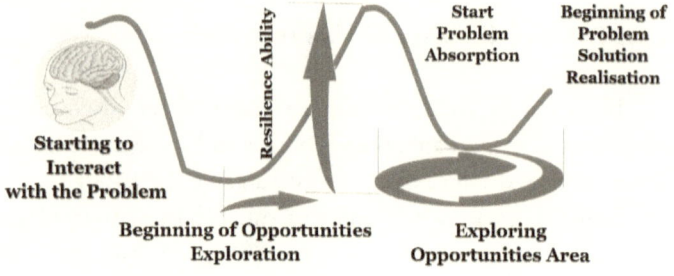

4.2.3 Social Applications of Nudges and Inspiration Economy

Nagatsu (2015) explored the use of social nudges in policy interventions that would induce voluntary cooperation in social dilemma situations which can be defended against two ethical objections that are the objections from coherence and autonomy. Thaler and Sunstein (2008) popularised libertarian paternalism, the idea that behavioural economics and psychology "the emerging science of choice" provides policymakers with new tools to influence people's economic and other choices for their own benefit without compromising their freedom of choice.

Nudges are subtle behavioural interventions that are distinct from standard regulations that operate with incentives. Sunstein (2015), Sugden (2009) and Sunstein and Thaler (2009). Although nudges have already been applied as behavioural public policy in a wide range of domains (Shafir 2013), nudge paternalism has attracted ethical and moral debate. IE labs have had many social applications in public, civil and private sector. For IE, coexistence and establishing effective social cohesion programmes can bring about more productive citizens that provide value-added to the broader community (Buheji, 2016). The observation of the current market setting in both Nudge and IE labs leads societies to go deeper in understanding individualistic behaviour. Buheji and Ahmed (2017a, b) and Nagatsu (2015).

4.2.4 Understanding the Economics of Trust

Covey (2006) seen that trust is the main issue in service complication and failure. Covey confirm that the availability of trust in the organisation process it can affect its speed and cost outcomes. When trust goes down, speed goes down and cost goes up. There are many examples in everyday life and in services delivery that shows how the issue of trust can influence our economic and socio-economic decisions, or obstruct it.

In health centres, the issue of patients' appointment and reaching the physicians' trust can be categorised to be societal-trust, self-trust and relationship-trust. This means it is a complicated problem that needs a behavioural change.

4.2.5 How BE and Inspiration Lab Work on Building Trust?

Trust between suppliers and customers is one of the main challenges that still face service industries in general and healthcare services specifically. Studies one of the ways to solve a complex problem like the lack of trust between the supplier and the customers change the environment or distract it.

Influencing the mindsets to make organisations and communities get more engaged to create a focused outcome (Hogg and Cooper, 2007; Mathieu et al., 2000). The level of influence can vary based on people engagement, level of distraction and the learning from the pilot (Buheji, 2016 and 2017). The work of Thaler and his colleagues also focus on influencing change through diverting people decision to what is believed to be towards their benefit.

In today busy life, we need to influence with minimal resources and the quick impact that can be felt by more people.

Both concepts of BE and IE labs use influencing without power as part of problem-solving and problem finding that lead to overcoming complexity and the creation of development.

Distraction is one of the most significant methodologies for inspiration, because when we are distracted, we are more prone to think outside of the problem. Overcoming distraction, or disruption can lead to an inspiration that leads to something real and tangible. Many scientists create an intentional psychological obstacle to stimulate the ability of their targeted beneficiaries to learn beyond the traditional environment.

Studies show that what prevents us from finding a solution is not a distraction, but rather a functional fixation. Therefore, we sometimes need to appreciate 'ill-structured problems', since in reality, they have more probability for creating a suitable engagement for learners. Even though 'ill-structured problems' start with fuzziness and distraction, they possess multiple solutions.

In relevant to building trust and useful communication model in health centres, both the techniques of BE and inspiration labs work together to reduce the uncertainty. The first step to reducing this uncertainty is interpreting the problem and synthesising the opportunities that the problem brings. The second step in dealing with the uncertainty of the problem is to capitalise on the opportunities exploited from the challenges of the problem or its characteristics to come up with new learnings that solve the problem. Tversky and Kahneman (1974).

Shaping social, environmental and economic decisions need shaking of the assumption of the stakeholders through behavioural and psychological factors. At the heart of these texts is a critique of economic theory which is based on rational assumptions; where social and behavioural factors matter, Ariely (2008) and Shiller (2005). However, one needs to take into account what Sugden (2009) concluded that humans make choices without 'full attention, perfect information, unimpaired cognitive ability and complete self-control'. Nagatsu (2015).

To establish more certainty, i.e. trust mindset, the cognitive process starts to stimulate the Prefrontal-Cortex, then the Anterior-Cingulate Cortex and then the Striatum, as illustrated in Figure (2). The hypothalamus (specifically Amygdala) helps to maintain the hormones homeostasis during the stages of building the trust throughout the field study, as shown in Figure (2). This help to maintain the body internal condition, despite changing external environment conditions due to the dynamics of the problem challenges. The problem investigation excites the Oxytocin which is secreted into the bloodstream, by the posterior pituitary gland. This help to enhance the management of the problem certainty where the electrical activity of the neurons would be regulated. Buheji (2018), Kahneman (2011), Tversky and Kahneman (1974).

Markman (2015) emphasise that there is many neuroscience research that is interested in the behavioural effects of oxytocin in increasing trust in humans. However, as Markman confirms later that this relation is not yet fully confirm and it still depends on preliminary evidence.

Figure (2) Areas of the Brain involved in Problem-solving

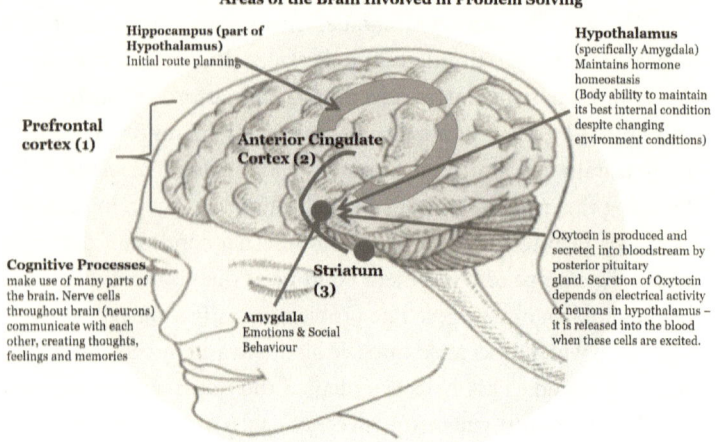

4.3 Application of Nudge and Inspiration Economy Labs in Health Centre Patient Prioritisation Scheme

4.3.1 The situation before the implementation of the project

Before applying the BE or ILs, the patients used to arrive at the Clinic (with or without appointment). Then they used to queue to take a number for registration; then they would have a waiting time for about 30 minutes. Then patients would be called for doctor clinic for diagnosis. Then the patient would go to the treatment room, or transferred for emergency clinic or directly transferred to the hospital by ambulance.

4.3.2 After the Implementation of the Project

The project started by adopting the following triage codes protocol in the piloted project:

Rad Code Case – where patients should see the physician in zero minutes,

Yellow Coded Case- where the patient needs treatment and should be seen in less than 30 minutes,

Green Code Case – where the patients need a check-up and they can wait for 30 minutes or more.

The project called 'Trust' where the health centre would pilot trusting the patients for the first time to code themselves. Five public health centres agreed to participate in such a project, and they were among the highest patients demands centres. Once the coding auto machine is set, the patients were directed to decide first their level of urgency to see the physician, i.e. to autonomously prioritise themselves. Based on the colour coded ticket, the sign and the steps direct the patient for either entering directly to the physician in the emergency room or set down for triage prioritisation if the yellow code is chosen.

The outcome of this piloted 'Trust' study showed that red patients that chosen red code were seen by physicians within 5 minutes in Emergency Room and there ten critical cases from all the five health centres that were considered complicated emergency cases that needed to be transferred to the hospital.

In a pilot of the five collaborating health centres and with the 'Trust' project run for one month only, more than 87% of the patients (19500) chosen Green code for their case. Only 12.7% chosen a yellow code and 0.35% only evaluated themselves as red, and they were all right. The project has shown that giving trust to patients to verify their condition reduced the load and risks of emergency patients being collapsed while waiting for the diagnosis. Figure (3) compares the influence of 'Trust' project in the streamlining of the patients' pathways.

Figure (3) Illustrate the Accessibility to Physicians before and after the 'Trust' project.

Patients satisfaction increased from 43%, seeing the service to be (very good), to more than 71% being satisfied (very good) after the project. Family physicians believe they are now more relaxed with patients as they trust the triage of the colours of green and yellow, while giving the most appropriate time for the patient instead of trying to giving them all 5 minutes regardless of the case, like used to be before. Nurses believe that now they have better communication with both the physicians and the patients and which reduced their stress by 20%.

The project revealed more data about red cases coming to the health centre and thus, improvement of the treatment protocol and resources. I.e. cases as chest pain, asthma, severe vomiting and diarrhea, bleeding, high blood pressure, very high diabetes, severe injuries or traumas and infants with high temperature are known to be red cases that patients would be comfortable to choose. The codification system also enhanced the interest of the medical team (the physicians and the nurses) in the peer-review.

According to BE and inspiration labs, this distraction to the process influenced the patients' behaviour in predictable ways, by changing their choice architecture. This intervention brought significant change to the socio-economic benefit of the patients and health services providers and reduced the risk of non-noticed emergency patients waiting for physician call by 90%.

4.4 Discussion

There are lots of learning that can be discussed from the 'Trust' project. Inspiration Labs using BE works to effectively inspires people to make more compassionate choices targeting social change. Life observations and reflections, as per IE labs would help people and organisation to see and visualise the big picture that to create better realisations of certain life, organisational or social challenges by turning them into opportunities. Through the practices of (Inspiration Engineering) the ability to challenge many status quo situations through distraction. This provides the organisation, or the community with rich opportunities for innovative ideas to follow and which usually are socially ignored or resisted.

The colour coding and giving patients the autonomous responsibility to decide about the priority of their case created a new level of accountability and different level and type of behavioural change amongst the patients and health centre staff. This created better capacity development and led to influence on the social welfare and created mindset change.

4.5 Conclusion and Recommendation

This chapter set a good practice of using BE and inspiration labs to re-building trust between supplier and customer in many service industries, including healthcare. The chapter shows the role of BE and IE labs for creating behavioural change outcomes.

The chapter also shows that their might many misperceptions or misconception about citizens biased judgement with they are given the autonomy of choice.

'The Trust Project' managed to illustrate a model of how we can improve lots of public services, such as having higher accessibility to healthcare services and thus reduce the morbidity and the mortality effect through simple, non-resource based behavioural techniques. Such projects not only reduce the malfunction in services designs, but also build healthier relations in the communities and within the organisation. This project could be studied further from the point of economically value-added outcome that came as a result of making more time for the family physicians and the nurses to focus on the patient diagnosis and treatment, rather than triaging and managing the patients' appointments system.

Since the chapter has shown the importance of autonomous codification on the public services in general and in healthcare specifically, the researcher recommends more work to be continued in this line. The chapter would have more benefits too on the services where cases of urgency are mixed up with standard cases. Due to the richness of the data available and the need to the improve many communities' services based on 'Trust' mindset and designs, more work empirical work is needed on how to build trust in specific decision-making points which would improve the quality of life of all the stakeholders. This would not only help better communication and quality of services, but even could save lives and have a drastic effect on our socio-economic outcome.

References

Ariely, D. (2008) Predictably Irrational: The Hidden Forces that Shape Our Decisions. London: Harper Collins.

Buheji, M (2018a) Re-inventing Our Lives- A Handbook for Socio-Economic Problem Solving, AuthorHouse, UK.

Buheji, M (2017) Understanding Problem Solving in Inspiration Labs, American Journal of Industrial and Business Management, 7, pp. 771-784,

Buheji, M and Ahmed, D (2017a) Breaking the Shield- Introduction to Inspiration Engineering: Philosophy, Practices and Success Stories, Archway Publishing, Simon & Schuster, USA.

Buheji, M and Ahmed, D (2017b) Understanding the Role of 'Inspiration Productivity, International Journal of Current Advanced Research Volume 6; Issue 3; April 2017; Page No. 2866-2871.

Buheji, M (2016) Handbook of Inspiration Economy. Bookboon.

Covey, S (2006) The SPEED of Trust: The One Thing that Changes Everything, Simon and Schuster, USA.

Hansen, P. (2016) The Definition of Nudge and Libertarian Paternalism: Does the Hand Fit the Glove? European Journal of Risk Regulation, 7(01), pp.18-20.

Kahneman, D (2011) Thinking, fast and slow. London: Macmillan.

Levitt, S. and List., J (2009) Field experiments in economics: the past, the present, and the future. European Economic Review, 53(1): 1–18.

Markman, A. (2015) Is Oxytocin the "Trust Molecule"? The effects of oxytocin on behaviour may not be so simple. Psychology Today.
https://www.psychologytoday.com/us/blog/ulterior-motives/201512/is-oxytocin-the-trust-molecule, Accessed on: 12/4/2018.

Nagatsu, M (2015) Social Nudges: Their Mechanisms and Justification, Review of Philosophy and Psychology, 6 (3), 481-494.

Sunstein, C.R. (2015) Nudges, agency, and abstraction: a reply to critics. Review of Philosophy and Psychology, 6, pp. 511–529.

Sugden, R (2009) On Nudging: A Review of Nudge: Improving Decisions About Health, Wealth and Happiness by Richard H. Thaler and Cass R. Sunstein, International Journal of the Economics of Business, Vol 16, Issue 3, Oct, pp 365-373. https://doi.org/10.1080/13571510903227064, Accessed: 12/4/2018.

Sunstein, C and Thaler, R (2009) Nudge: Improving Decisions About Health, Wealth and Happiness. 1st ed.

Tinkler, J. (2011) Designing for Nudge Effects: how behaviour management can ease public sector problems.

Tversky, A. and Kahneman, D. (1974) Judgment under Uncertainty: Heuristics and Biases. Science, 185(4157), pp.1124-1131.

CHAPTER THREE

Behavioural Economics Trends in Improving Governments Outcomes – Much more than Nudge[3]

3.1 Introduction

The goal of public services and the deployment of government policies is to shape societal behaviours. Government services, however, have a specificity that needs to be reflected in its models. Today, with the spread of BE Labs government entities can benefit from the environment that helps to capture opportunities and enhance the economic actors.

In this empirical research, the differentiation between outcomes that are based on reasoning and field experience is contrasted.

---

[3] Buheji, M. (2018) Behavioural Economics Trends in Improving Governments Outcomes – Much More than Nudge, American Journal of Economics, 8(3): 163-173

In this chapter, the researcher shall compare all the characteristics of Nudge to Inspiration Economy Labs (IL's) with a specific focus on welfare services that influence the quality of life without extra resources or without the need of power or authority. The BE models are explored whether both would improve governments productivity and outcome. The methodology target to consider whether both concepts can be methodologies for future waves of government transformation.

The method of inquiry through "typical observations" or "experiments through observation" that leads to a differentiated mindset are reviewed to gather more profound evidence of similarities and differentiation. Actual empirical methods of inquiry (i.e. experiments, observations) are done in a comparative study. The comparative study here focuses only on social welfare and quality of life services in order to keep the focus on the BE role in creating differentiated outcomes and shaping the positive behaviours and the mindset of the communities with minimal resources. Therefore, the inter-related services such as Social Insurance (Pension Fund), Social Development and Healthcare Services are compared. This chapter can be further developed in the future to show how utilising BE models can help create more radical changes in government services. Buheji and Ahmed (2018), Chetty (2015), Samson (2015), Dolan et al. (2010).

3.2   3. Literature Review

3.2.1 Role of Governments in Shaping the Behaviours

Government central role in the development of a nation. Therefore, each utmost government focus is on stabilising the overall socio-economic conditions and then to regulate such behaviour to achieve its both economic and social goals through services that would make continuous development for the citizen and the businesses. This can be achieved only through empirical scientific research and field research. Buheji (2016), Blanding (2017), Dolan et al. (2010).

Different government programs in the United Kingdom, the United States, Australia, Canada, Denmark, France and Singapore are pushing the decision-makers to experiment and explore the intentional use of BE in social policy, Thaler and Sunstein (2008). In the small island of the Kingdom of Bahrain, another type of BE labs called inspiration labs had been experimented in different government entities, also targeting more profound socio-economic outcomes. The Economist (2012), Jahrami and Buheji (2012), Keating (2013), Chetty (2015).

3.2.2 Specificity of Government Services

The breadth of their powers characterises government organisations compared to other sectors. Part of differentiated government power is their capacity to propose and enforce citizens. However, the main role of any government entity is to deliver services that improve the quality of life, ensure fairness of the welfare system while ensuring socio-economic development.

Government entities might lose the essence of their existence, especially when they operate in a market-based economy where they focus on satisfying certain conditions relating to their governance and operating conditions rather than the outcome of their services delivery.

Even though government organisations have the authority to make and enforce decisions on society, they usually cannot manage to change people decisions easily. Thaler and Sunstein (2008).

Government organisation jurisdiction extends to all members of the community physical force and coercion. The political legitimacy of developed governments comes not only from their services, but from the outcome achieved.

3.2.3 Introduction to Behavioral Economics

BE today is becoming a more stable branch of economics and management and started to incorporates the best alternatives of field experimentation and solutions of human problems from different perspectives. BE targets to help create better life model outcome that may have not been exposed or predicted before. Buheji (2017), Dolan et al. (2010), Thaler and Sunstein (2008).

Government BE models are built around cognitive rationality that reduces the risk and uncertainty. Such BE models come as a result of focused labs attempt that target to identify systematic biases in a specific area. This eagerness and drive to create models are improving the government curiosity towards using scientific approaches to develop testable hypotheses and predict socio-economic behaviors. This can be seen clearly in Nudge projects. McAuley (2007).

BE also fits the efforts that comes from inspirational observational learning that create practical application of mirror neurons which its existence hints the brain-behavioural link. The integration different intentional learning helps to improve the government entity capacity to adapt new environments and integrate knowledge from different inspiration sources. Samson (2015).

Inspiration labs (ILs) uses intentional integrative learning to build different government connections that seemingly bring in disparate information that create better decisions. ILs exploration journey in government entities help to diagnose the community learning needs, i.e. study the type of citizens' attitudes and behaviours that would formulate the learning goals and outcomes. **Blanding (2017) and** Buheji and Ahmed, (2017a).

The objective of this chapter is to explore how two BE techniques one is becoming globally known and called Nudge and the other is just emerging in limited government practices called Inspiration Labs (IL's) are leading to better government services outcomes with more efficient alternatives. Both techniques have their own way of exploring and exploiting on opportunities and building model that leads to behavioural change or architecting decisions with less bureaucratic approaches. While Nudge depends on the small changes to the "choice environment" can encourage large changes in people's actions, IL's depends on discovering hidden opportunities and capitalising on them to create major leap without extra resources. Both ways are very useful for governments and government organisation that are serious towards creating legacy. Buheji and Ahmed (2018), **Blanding (2017),** Samson (2015), Sunstein (2014), Thaler and Sunstein (2008).

3.2.4 BE Labs role in Government Service Development

Thaler and Sunstein (2008) seen that nudge in services as in government would play like a choice architecture that alters behaviour in a predictable way without forbidding any options, or significantly changing their economic incentives.

Since government services is very important for any society development, BE labs are considered one of the best accelerators for achieving this development since it addresses cultural dynamical needs. This is why Nobel psychologist Daniel Kahneman sees that what is called government BE is in fact social psychology. A growing body of evidence demonstrates that behavioural science research findings help to make effective direction that would improve government policies. Samson (2015), Dolan et al (2010).

The core questions of BE labs therefore focus on why the government services are delivered without a foreseen outcome? Can't they really solve the problem? Have they try to see the way or the mindset in which the current services are delivered and have they tried to change it? What type of hidden opportunities did the government tried to discover? What are the values, strategies and practice that the government managed to change to improve and develop its targeted socio-economic outcomes? Sunstein (2014).

3.2.5 Capturing Opportunities through BE Models

BE help to create a pull thinking in government decision making process. This specifically can be seen when government decides where to capture opportunities to create the targeted behavioural change. Thaler and Sunstein (2008).

Governments once started to collect the possible opportunities they would usually manage to link between the pieces of information using different observational analysis techniques and type of thinking that focus on the essence of the service itself. This type of thinking helps them to see or visualise the future and thus weight the present benefits or costs compared to the future benefits or costs. For example, many government spends millions of dollars annually on encouraging people to take flu prevention shots to reduce absenteeism, however one could see opportunities in people not attending to such vaccination for specific demographics and explore techniques that would alter those vulnerable of further condition or diseases if they catch the flu. Sunstein (2013)

Once the government entity build passion about the essence of the services they deliver to the extent they would do this codification and classification, then they could build a holistic understanding of the process of change and move towards finding a measured outcome. Government would then use the models to change its people assumptions and enhance their involvement.

3.2.6 BE and Government Economic Actors

BE focus on government economic actors to improve the society wellbeing and future generations. Economic actors of government entities use mechanics of the economics to enhance different factors that influence the way people behave and interact when they are engaged in economic activities. Samson (2015). Therefore, in earlier research inspiring governments were characterised as those that have the capacity to use the different socio-economic actors to develop services and products that would meet best outcome and the purpose of their existence, where Buheji (2016) called it an End-Customer-End. i.e. The ultimate goal of any excellent, inspiring government service.

Governments almost design their citizens services and measure it by cost or volume. Hence, usually their business models is designed based on focus of what is perceived is good for the citizens, as shown Figure (1). While BE labs work on creating citizens services that are measured by value where the business model is focused on the value that addresses real citizens needs. Buheji (2016), Sunstein (2013).

Figure (1) Government Transformation when Influenced by BE actors

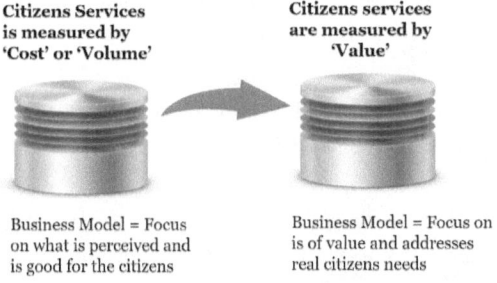

Buheji and Ahmed (2017) mentioned that behavioural inspirational model influence would not only help in developing emotional connections, but goes also towards changing attitudes that will enhance the culture of communication, collaboration and innovation, thus leading to realised change. The model focuses on achieving the end-result; it clearly illustrates what the organisation expects and inspires others to achieve higher performance level. Hence such BE models would also help the government organisations to see the big picture and build a clear view of the future.

Behavioural inspirational model could also create energy and excitement in the workplace, as it would involve the stakeholders using pull-thinking techniques that enhance passion towards bringing in focused initiatives or improve the capacity of solving problems. Customers can play a great role in being another inspirational source.

Government BE actors could start with the disruptive questions, such as questioning what business we are in, while observing the visualised target, the End-Customer-End mindset would work effectively. This type of thinking would turn government organisations to be more consumer-driven; where their products, services and solutions would be grounded around consumers' needs. Buheji (2017), Thaler (2015).

Therefore, one could consider that the maturity of any government organisation today is no longer measured by its years in business, but rather by its experience of creating an environment of fulfilling the End-Customer-End visualisation through adopting more BE designed tools and practices.

3.2.7 Comparing spirit of Nudge vs. Inspiration Economy Approaches and Projects

BE is a multi-disciplined concept that explore and then architect the behaviour of the organisation and the people to deliver better outcomes. For example, behavioural scientists focus on architecting designs when Nudging to specific needs to have auto Opt-In or Opt-Out in order to transform specific government challenges and/or speed up towards a designed outcome that would build later success stories. Sunstein (2014) Thaler (2015).

IE Labs even though they focus too on architecting the essence of government service designs, they target actually to change the government services outcomes through changing the mindset and the assumptions that these services were built on. The uniqueness here is that this change doesn't depend first on systems and standards, but on people involvement through collections of observations that focus on higher availability and capacity to discover the intrinsic powers within. Once the opportunities are exploited through realised models then the results of IL's project are generalised. Buheji (2018a).

Both BE techniques have their unique spirits. This is due to the way they are differentiated in their delivery. Synthesis of the work of Thaler and Sunstein (2008) and Buheji and Ahmed (2017a) the following could be seen in comparing Nudge vs. Inspiration Labs. Nudge would focus mostly on exploring the government service business objectives, improving it choices dimension and implementing behavioural concepts through promoting and mitigating risks, as shown in Figure (2). While IL's would depend on visualisation of the essence of the government services that is usually followed by a curiosity spirit that comes from exploring of the opportunities and building models that are generalised to show the influence positive change. In order for both BE techniques to reach their targets, continuous adjustment of biases artefacts towards the targeted outcomes,

Figure (2) Flow of Spirit of Nudge vs. Inspiration Labs towards Targeted Outcome.

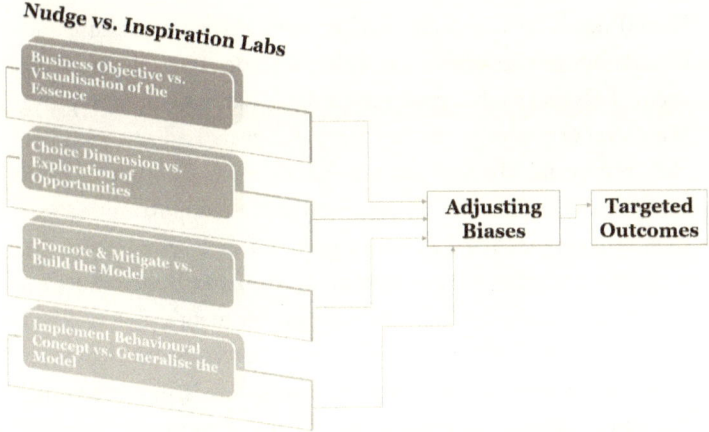

3.2.8 BE Success Stories in Changing Government Outcomes

Once the BE government models achieve its targeted outcomes, the policymaker should consider seeing how to link between the choices and eliminate any negative or unpopular results from the community, or from the government partners. Some governments would use public feedback to shape their next behavioural interventions. However, most governments would study the effect of these interventions in order to calibrate their processes and procedures where necessary. The Economist (2012), Buheji (2016), Chetty (2015), Dolan et al (2010).

Studies of Thaler and Sunstein (2008) and Buheji and Ahmed (2017a) shows that BE techniques are very suitable for government services if it managed to promote people's health, safety or welfare, but without compromising, or manipulating people goals or interests or values. Actually, the focus on either BE techniques bring more scientific approaches inside the government culture.

Success stories in government organisation as reported by Jahrami and Buheji (2012) and earlier by Thaler and Sunstein (2008) needs governments that can use choice architecture and default options to encourage citizens to do what is better for them. This means that government organisations would improve their level of communications to what is visualised as a moral or civic responsibilities not just services delivery. The role of each government entity would then be to explore opportunities and then help people to make better choices for themselves, or for the betterment of their society. Sunstein (2013) and Buheji (2016).

In the United Kingdom, the government's Behavioural Insights Team (BIT) work on creating success stories through applying Nudge economics practices to policy issues. More and more behavioural scientists are involved in government services design and are implementing nudges to steer citizens' decisions away from what is 'bad' towards what is 'good' for the individual or the society, Chetty (2015), Samson (2015), Sunstein (2014), Dolan et al (2010), McAuley (2007).

3.2.9 Building the Government Service BE Models

This chapter tries to recognize the current BE government models with focus on Nudge and IE. Both BE labs work through government teams to improve government effectiveness, or efficiency, leading to better government service innovation. Building such government models would help to build new services that improve outcomes at best operational costs. Buheji (2016), McAuley (2007).

Government BE models are generalised when they manage to create positive behaviour change besides when they influence people lives, Buheji (2018b). For example, through Nudge, organ donations are simply changed to be the default option same as the retirement savings plans which leads to an enormous uptick in the numbers who participate and amounts saved. In another example models that target to change citizens' behaviour through encouraging payment of traffic tickets are delivered by violators letter that carries "Pay Now" in red letters at the top where photos of traffic camera is sent too in the letter. Sunstein (2014).

There are many types of BE models that are suitable for government services, however here only two types are discussed, Nudge and IL's based models. Nudge models are designed to change behaviours through manipulating people decision. For example, redesigning the hospital ads reminders from "Hand Hygiene prevents you from catching diseases" by replacing the word (you) with (patients); i.e. to make it read as "Hand Hygiene prevents patients from catching diseases". This simple change found to encourage physicians and patients to wash hands effectively. While IL's models are designed to change people mindset which behavior is one of its components through raising the stakeholders' capacity to discover hidden opportunities. For example, IL's would to find opportunities to enhance patients discharge to avoid stagnation of beds and protect patients from getting infection due to length of stay. Sunstein (2014), Buheji (2018a), Dolan et al (2010), Thaler and Sunstein (2008).

Both models would have an influence on the society while improving the socio-economic outcome. The first model would help to increase those who use the soap and handwashing, thus reducing cross-infection, while the second model would help towards giving more priority and fairness for those patients that need the bed most. Buheji (2018b).

BE models in government Inspiration labs (IL's) are created through effective learning techniques that help to change the mindset and its explored intrinsic powers. Both Nudge and IL's create their models through exploring, assembling, composing, constructing, creating, designing, developing, formulating, organizing, analysing and proposing practices that would help to come up with the best suitable inspiration reference for the society, Buheji (2018a). Government can deliver solutions to specific community phenomenon or behaviours through exactly describing, or indicating, or restating, re-translating, or re-arranging, re-defining, re-labelling, or re-producing specific solutions that create a nudge or inspiration that is reflected in overcoming the complexity of the problem or the challenge tackled. **Blanding (2017),** Buheji (2017), Dolan et al (2010).

However, if we study the inspiration models well see they are organised first by knowledge capturing and dissemination. The BE models in IE use the available resources, or with minimal resources. The models are usually designed to allow individuals to interact with their environment. Buheji and Ahmed (2017a).

Hence, government entities would build models based on different qualitative and quantitate studies that show specific pattern recognitions.

For example, through IL's government can re-invent the business models to address many chronic issues in the society that accumulated after the service design and delivery. Same would happen with Nudge, when observing interactions of the way services are delivered. Buheji (2016), Thaler (2015).

3.2.10 Welfare Analysis in Behavioral Models

Dealing with mindset goes beyond the economist arguments rational or irrational behaviours and/or its influence techniques on public policy or services development. Therefore, dealing with assumption, attitudes and behaviours in government services should be still the most important aim and should be more examined through the lens of multi-disciplined social scientists. Actually, it should go beyond the academic circles, especially if BE models are to tackle complex issues as improvement of a country's quality of life and welfare system. Chetty (2015), Keating (2013).

Role of developed governments is to establish a welfare system and quality of life net that would determine the best optimal policy that would deal with the possibilities of behavioral biases. With the turbulent socio-economic environment, contemporary time have shown that the challenges to social welfare programs does not depends only on governments experiences in dealing with the welfare issues only, but on how governments can practically tackle the consistent behavioral change and challenges. Buheji (2016) and Sunstein (2014).

3.2.11 Role of BE in Government Services Productivity

According to their analysis, money spent on nudges can in some cases be more than 40 times more effective than the next most effective method, a dramatic result for governments dealing with scarce resources. Chetty (2015).

Buheji and Ahmed (2017b) emphasis that the outcome of government productivity is beyond quantitative returns as it is very high compared to 'the Return on Capital Employed'. As besides its delivered differentiated outcome in relevance to the essence of the existence of the government service, IL's also manage to improve the government entities culture towards being more proactive and very efficient in their hit rate and in dealing or solving different issues.

Today, one could hear more behavioural teams are formed as part of ministerial and/or state level. These scientific teams provide not only strategic guidance for the government, but in fact work on capacity building through innovation lab and rigorous testing in relevance to citizens' behavioural characteristics and required change.

3.3 Methodology

The scientific process of hypothetico-deductive model is utilised to compare two different approaches of BE, namely Nudge vs. IE Labs (called IL's). The sequence of the observation and the experimentation and then the influence of both approaches are reviewed to generate similarities and differences. The methods of inquiry through observations and/or experiments and how they influence the government mindset are reviewed in literature and then compared to gather evidence of similarities and differentiations. Actual empirical methods of inquiry (i.e. experiments, observations) are done in a comparative study.

Due to the limitation and the feasibility of this research paper Government Social Welfare and Quality of Life Service are used to further specify the scope of comparison. A separate list for both Nudge and Inspiration Labs are done ensure effective understanding about the type of field experiment and what is the outcome expected.

Careful focused discussion and analysis targeted to mainly see the differentiation between the approaches of Nudge and IL's. Since Behaviour economics believe in the scientific principles of determinism and orderliness and in what likely to respond as a result, an attempt towards understanding of what happens to the mindset of the government organisations when experiments and observations are carried out in a certain sequence is explored.

The scientific approach to the unobserved influence without power or with minimal resources is studied in both Nudge and IL's process as per an earlier work of Buheji (2018b). Full understanding, prediction of both approaches complexity of environment and outcomes are studied too.

3.4 Comparative Study

3.4.1 Purpose of this Comparative Study

From the recent literature reviewed in this chapter we can see clearly that leading governments are becoming more aware about the importance of BE in creating a positive change in society. However, there is still huge literature gap that need to address how governments can use BE techniques other than nudge, in order to create behavioural change for complex issues as social welfare that would lead to better quality of life. Therefore, the following comparison target to focus only on three main sectors that any developed or developing government would consider it as part of its main service responsibilities and be most accountable towards it as would be presented later in Tables (1) and (2).

3.4.2 Government Social Welfare and Quality of Life Service

Most important needs for any society is to improve the quality of life of its citizens and specially for the most vulnerable ones through focusing first on the effectiveness of the social welfare services delivered and what is relevant to quality of life. Today, literature have enough data to explore the different BE projects carried out by governments with the intention of improving the outcomes of social development. Therefore, the comparison tables (1) and (2) in this study targets to focus mainly on projects related to inter-related services of Social Insurance (Pension Fund), Social Development and Healthcare Services. Buheji (2016) and Sunstein (2014).

In certain highly developed countries as Norway, the social security system is linked with processes of pension, social welfare and healthcare services to help improve the return-to-work outcomes. An example of the benefit of integrating these services is illustrated through the return of holding just one meeting between the employee, the employer, and the treating physician. The behavioural move of just holding such meetings led to enhance the employees returning to their job 10 days faster than those that didn't get such service. Keating (2013).

Since almost all governments spend lots huge time and money annually in dealing with vulnerable cases or in caring or treating people and most of the time get involved with problems that could've been preventable, BE comes as a highly alternative solution to deal with such environment. Therefore, the following tables (1) and (2) give example of the published work of both BE techniques under study Nudge and IL's for the three services that are considered one of the main pillars for social welfare that usually lead to better quality of life in any community or country.

3.4.3 Nudge List

Table (1) Selected Nudge List in Government Social Welfare Services that leads to Quality of Life

Type of Government Services	Nudge Success Stories
Social Insurance (Pension Fund) Keating (2013) Sunstein (2014) Thaler (2015) Thaler and Sunstein (2008)	Private Sector employees not enrolling in Pension Fund Government designed an Auto Enrolment (Opt-In) for Pension for all Private Sector Employee with provision for Opt-Out only based on request.
Social Development Keating (2013) Thaler and Sunstein (2008)	People are not Saving Government would provide Envelops to the poor family to encourage savings (with their Children Photo on it).
Healthcare Services Keating (2013) Sunstein (2014) Thaler (2015) Thaler and Sunstein (2008)	Organ Donations There is currently a lack of organ donors in many countries. One way to increase the number of organ donors' government introduced automatic enrollment (Opt-In) for all the people, i.e. all the citizens are considered organ donors unless otherwise specified to (Opt-Out). Encouraging Walking Decisions To reduce Obesity and Cardio-Vascular Diseases, people are encouraged to exercise more, i.e. as in putting walking steps towards the stair case, instead towards the lift. Nudging Smoking Habits To more clearly show the negative effects of smoking, many countries have started to add deterrent pictures on the cigarette packages with images that display damaged organs that can be a consequence of long term smoking. This is meant to discourage people to start smoking and motivate people that are smokers to quit.

Type of Government Services	Nudge Success Stories
	Nudging towards Healthy Food
Since overconsumption of calorie rich food can lead to a deteriorating health, governments are attempting to get employees to eat healthier, through rearranging the cafeteria and supermarkets. Healthy food are to be placed at eye-level and easily available for the visitors of the cafeteria. Unhealthy food, such as candy or snacks was placed behind the counter to make them less visible and accessible for the visitors in the cafeteria. The idea with this intervention is to encourage the consumption of healthier alternatives to improve the health of the citizens.

Nudging Medication Decisions
Patients are motivated to adherence to take their heart medication, especially in chronic diseases, on time even if they do not experience any symptoms by employing a combination of small financial incentives for scheduling cholesterol appointments ($5 gift cards or lottery draw) along with a type of (Post-it note reminders) describing the consequences of not taking the medication. This strict adherence to medications reduced emergency room visits and hospitalizations by 30%.

Reduction of Medical Treatment Cost through increasing Generic Drugs Prescriptions
Prescription of expensive brand-name rather than generic drugs is nudged through an electronic medical system that is defaulted to give the equivalent generic drug when the drug brand name is typed. To override this default, i.e. keep the brand name for certain patients, the prescribing doctor need to check a box labeled "dispense as written." |

3.4.4 Inspiration Labs List

Table (2) Selected Inspiration Labs List in Government Social Welfare Services that leads to Quality of Life

Type of Government Services	Inspiring Labs Process
Social Insurance (Pension Fund) Buheji and Ahmed (2017a);	-In order to attract more participants to pension fund, the government started a lab for selective investment of pension fund that would enhance the productivity of the national economy and Local Market Stability -Develop pension fund for social responsibility where lower pension participants are more prepared for entrepreneurship after retirement.
Social Development Buheji and Ahmed (2017a)	-Improving the Quality of Life of the Elderly and the Geriatric Care Homes through exploring the human and social asset intrinsic powers ability. -Improving the capacity of the productive family program to be more self-independent and attractive for more family members to join as full time employees/ owners -Building stronger family businesses that have higher Return on Capital Employed (ROCE). -Enhance the return from Elderly homecare production -Enhance the quality of Disabled Production
Healthcare Services Primary Care Buheji and Ahmed (2017a)	Early detection of Non Communicable Diseases (NCD's) (Diabetes, Blood Pressure, Cholesterol and Obesity) Enhancement of Quality of life through development of Families Physicians team program Practicing Triage to establish priority cases system

Type of Government Services	Inspiring Labs Process
	Early detection of Psycho-Somatic in relevance to Anxiety in Health Centre. Optimising the role of Social Workers and Health Educational Specialist and Health visitors in family screening Enhancing patients time spent with physicians
Healthcare Services Secondary Care (Hospitals) Buheji and Ahmed (2017a)	Improving the total throughput in Accident & Emergency and admissions in Hospitals based on Urgency of the cases Enhancing the availability of the Capacity of Beds Utilisation by inspiring towards higher discharges on time and based on defined protocols & followup services Reduction in Antibiotics prescription and use in main referral hospital
Healthcare Services Public Health Buheji and Ahmed (2017a)	-Establishing 'Intelligent Inspection' that minimize the rate of poisonous calls or low hygiene fines by 90% with less manpower resources & trust worthiness enhancement. -Enhancement of reputation of fast food services that supports local tourism. -Intelligent inspection based on pull thinking and lean management that enhanced the outcome of hospitality services and with minimal resources.
Healthcare Services Health Enrichment Buheji and Ahmed (2017a)	Enhancement of 'Quality of Life' practices & style in coordination with Health Centres
Healthcare Services Psychiatric Services Buheji and Ahmed (2017a)	-Improving the self and healthcentres capacity to manage the anxiety to avoid reaching the level of chronic anxiety -Reduce the need to treat anxiety with medicines. -Reduce suicide ratio due to early treatment of main causalities among youth. -Reduce the patients sick leave due to self-assessments of psycho-sematic symptoms

3.5 6. Discussion

3.5.1 Way Data Being Collected before taking the Countermeasures.

From literature reviewed and the comparative tables, both concepts Nudge and IL's capitalise on collecting on observation and experimentation before setting the final countermeasure. However, IL's seems not to have any pre-judgement of what should be the countermeasure, while Nudge would have a different hypothesis that would be tested by people reaction. IL's would depend on the results of the field observation and impulses that challenge the mindset while exploring the explicit or hidden opportunities in relevance to a value-based visualisation.

The argument can be clarified with time, as with time more pieces of evidence of what happens to service organisations, as governments, when experiments and observations are carried out in a specific sequence. i.e. what happens to the mindset of the government when they do Nudge or IL's, which one is more effective. Even though this comparative data does not cover this issue in detail, it is considered an early attempt to see the big picture of the outcome of such BE projects or approaches.

3.5.2 Characteristics of Deploying BE techniques in Government Services

From the comparative tables (1) and (2), and the literature reviewed, one could notice that Nudge and IL's focus on governments doing something to create citizens behavioural change. According to behavioural scientists, such BE projects or labs is suitable for both the government and society. Chetty (2015), Dolan (2010).

However, the two BE techniques can be clearly differentiated in the way they tackle their projects. As shown in Figure (3), Nudge projects which are usually led by behavioural scientists in Nudge

Units, would usually start with the selection of scope of the choice architecture which is represented by for example setting the citizens choices for Opt-in or Opt-Out. This cause more acceptance and higher availability that leads to better government outcomes and success stories. The flow is from top to down, i.e. from government top management decision-makers to the beneficiaries of the services.

While as per Figure (3) the IE labs projects would start exploring opportunities from the field, i.e. where the beneficiaries would be ensured that the essence of the government services is addressed. The first behavioural change towards this level of mutual agreement starts with involving the concerned parties in discovering the opportunities and then turning it into a realised state through building a model that target specific outcome. Here the government top management would work on generalising the model and creating a governmental success story that can inspire other entities to try to replicate the model. Buheji and Ahmed (2018).

Figure (3) Characteristics of Nudge and IL's in Creating Government Services Success Stories

6.3 Process of Exploring Opportunities of BE Change

Coming back to the literature and comparative tables (1) and (2), shows that both Nudge and IL's create a type of codification first that help to absorb better the scope of the alternative business model that was not foreseen in the scope of the government service under study. Both, Nudge and IL's, would also start a classification process where they would be able to develop further the capability of interactions of the people involved through piloting the proposed solutions in different setting and environment.

When the BE process is carefully evaluated for both Nudge and IL's, one could see a clear differentiation as shown in Figure (4) where both Nudge and IL's goes through similar first two steps of their process, i.e. during observation and exploration of the opportunities that would bring in the behavioural change. However, based on both the literature reviewed and the comparative tables there is no clear evidence that Nudge would go further than this point, i.e. it would stop at the end of exploration point to take actions about the proposed behavioural pattern that would be disrupted. While if we study the cases of IL's we would see more steps are taken to help continue to create BE model through power of 'learning by doing' that would help to generalise its outcomes later. This differentiation of IL's from Nudge helps to develop the stakeholders mindset further and influence their capacity to reflect and visualise the best opportunities effectively. Thaler (2015), Buheji and Ahmed (2018). It is believed therefore that IL's seem to give the government entity more capability to stratify complex problems compared to Nudge.

Figure (4) BE Development process and where both Approaches of Nudge and Inspiration Labs meet and differentiate.

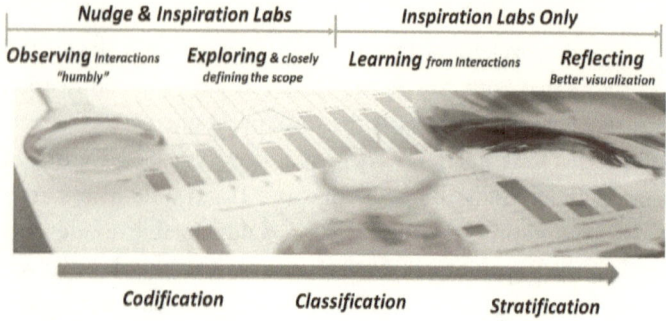

3.6 Conclusion

When BE models are alive in the targeted government organisation, they would be more competent to confront adversity, or challenges that are faced by or reflected on the beneficiaries. Positive BE models create empowering waves that prepare the government organisation or the community to develop their capacity in comparison with the expected demands.

Both BE techniques in this study found to be superior in specific characteristics when their influence on government services are compared from the specific scope as a welfare system that leads to a better quality of life. Nudge is found to be faster and simpler for government programs, but IL's create more effective and deeper mindset changes.

At the end of the day, BE is considered now a clearly unique development opportunity for all government entities. Recognition of BE programs means that government should optimise the spirit of scientific exploration that come when investigation on the type of behavioural change start to deliver opportunities for best outcomes. Great government transformation could occur if BE is systematically applied and the benefit of this multi-disciplined field is institutionalised in its culture.

Government organisations now have more excellent choices in solving chronic issues in many essential areas while also being able more to promote socially desirable citizens' behaviours. For example, Nudge could be used to encourage the participation of positive behaviours that would enhance the social welfare, while IL's could be used more to solve chronic problems that could not be solved with such behaviours, or it would need time or resources if to be solved. Both techniques would help to build some proactive government entities and better citizenship that brings in welfare measures before problems occur over time.

Even though the comparative data in this study does not give a clear cut about the effectiveness of the sequence of field experiments and observations on the mindset of the government organisation, i.e. whether the way of Nudge or IL's would influence the mindset more; this research can be considered an early attempt to see the big picture of the outcome of such BE approaches. The study shows that there are more BE approaches for improving government outcomes than just Nudge. Therefore, governments are highly recommended to keep up the new spirit of BE curiosity, but also be open-minded to try techniques as Inspiration Labs in order to create new cultures that can see variety of solutions to problems and still with most efficient way.

The objectivity in this research is optimised against any sources of bias related to personal experience or subjective ideas. However, in order to avoid any potential biases of the researcher influences due to his personal feelings and experiences, more studies are recommended in this line, i.e. comparing Nudge with similar BE driven field experiment labs, and in different countries and in variety of fields as done in this study, i.e. in healthcare, or education, etc. Studies as observing the government and citizens' behaviours after such BE approaches are highly recommended too.

References

Blanding, M (2017) Why Government 'Nudges' Motivate Good Citizen Behaviour, HBR.

Buheji, M (2018a) Nudge Theory vs Inspiration Economy Labs- Comparing the Depth of Influence on Socio-Economics Behaviours, American Journal of Economics; Vol. 8, No.3: 146-154

Buheji, M (2018b) "Influencing without Power" Currency in Inspiration Labs—A Case Study of Hospital Emergency Beds. American Journal of Industrial and Business Management, Vol. 8, pp. 207-220.

Buheji, M (2017) Understanding Problem-Solving in Inspiration Labs, American Journal of Industrial and Business Management, 7, pp. 771-784.

Buheji, M (2016) Inspiring Governments. LAP LAMBERT Academic Publishing.

Buheji, M and Ahmed, D (2018) Exploring Inspiration Economy, AuthorHouse, UK.

Buheji, M and Ahmed, D (2017a) Breaking the Shield- Introduction to Inspiration Engineering: Philosophy, Practices and Success Stories, Archway Publishing, FROM SIMON & SCHUSTER, USA.

Buheji, M and Ahmed, D (2017b) Understanding the Role of 'Inspiration Productivity', International Journal of Current Advanced Research Volume 6; Issue 3; April 2017; Page No. 2866-2871.

Chetty, R (2015) Behavioural Economics and Public Policy - A Pragmatic Perspective, American Economic Review, American Economic Association, vol. 105(5), pages 1-33, May.

Dolan, P; Hallsworth, M; Halpern, D and King, D (2010) MINDSPACE Influencing behavior through public policy, Institute for Government, Cabinet Office, https://www.instituteforgovernment.org.uk/sites/default/files/publications/MINDSPACE.pdf, Accessed on: 1/12/2017

Jahrami, H and Buheji, M (2012) Reporting a Success Story in the Context of Public Sector: Factors That Matters, Journal of Public Administration and Governance, Vol (2):3, pp. 96-103 http://www.macrothink.org/journal/index.php/jpag/article/view/2470, Accessed on: 1/12/2017

Kahneman, D (2011) Thinking Fast and Slow, FSG

Keating, J (2013) The Nudgy State. How five governments are using BE to encourage citizens to do right thing. https://www.instituteforgovernment.org.uk/sites/default/files/publications/MINDSPACE.pdf, Accessed on: 1/12/2017

McAuley, I (2007) BE and Public Policy: Some Insights, Working Paper http://www.home.netspeed.com.au/mcau/academic/bepubpol.pdf, Accessed on: 1/12/2017

Samson, A (2015) The BE Guide, http://www.behavioraleconomics.com., Accessed on: 1/12/2017

Sunstein, C (2013) Simpler: The Future of Government, Simon & Schuster.

Sunstein, C (2014) Why Nudge? The Politics of Libertarian Paternalism, Yale University Press.

Thaler, R (2015) Misbehaving, The Making of BE.

Thaler, R and Sunstein, C (2008) The Nudge, Improving Decisions About Health, Wealth and Happiness, Yale University Press.

The Economist (2012) Nudge Nudge, Think Think. The BE use in public policy shows promise, March http://www.economist.com/node/21551032, Accessed on: 1/12/2017

CHAPTER FOUR

Re-Inventing Public Services Using Gamification Approaches[4]

4.1 Introduction

Gamification is radical change approach which focuses on raising the capacity of the organisation and enhance its strength as conceptual models through fostering its intrinsic motivation in non-game contexts. Deci and Ryan (1985). This chapter investigates how gamification can help in creating change and re-inventing the public services in any country, taking the context of the Kingdom of Bahrain. Buheji (2019a), Buheji (2018), McGonigal (2011).

The approaches of the gamification in this chapter focus on developing government services delivery through depending on observations of available services and seeing how to create processes that would induce the involvement and engagement of the people. Velten (2017), Chin (2016).

---

[4] Buheji, M (2019) Re-Inventing Public Services Using Gamification Approaches, International Journal of Economics and Financial Issue 9(6): 48-59.

A review of the different game designs indicators is done after reviewing the concept of gamification and its critical success factors. After that, different motivational perspectives are analysed. Then psychology of gamification design is discussed. Sailer et al. (2013), Heckhausen and Heckhausen (2008), Deci and Ryan (1985).

The theoretical review results are compared to the effectiveness of the re-invented public services design, Werbach and Hunter (2012). Gamification in changing public services is to use its motivational power and environment influencing behaviour to foster better learning and awareness. This influence psychological perspective. Buheji (2019a), Deci and Ryan (1985).

4.2 Literature Review

4.2.1 Defining Gamification and what differentiates it

Gamification is about the application of any or all the elements of game playing or design (e.g., point scoring, competition with others, rules of play) to other areas of activity.

Gamification has evolved from the integration of the technological game designs and the social sciences. This integration has taken many phases of transformation until gamification became part of the socio-economic transformations thinking. Today gamification has become a proactive approach of how social involvement systems can be constructed. Madrid and Hunter (2012).

Gamification helps to turn a routine into something exciting through developing better interaction. By turning events into games, we can change many regular tasks into something exciting, and make it easier to learn or sustain a behaviour too. This can be very beneficial for social change. Landers et al. (2015), Rughiniş

(2013), McGonigal (2011), Deterding et al. (2011), Deterding et al. (2013).

Gamification is a method that applies the principles of games, and games design approaches into real-life activities, Kapp (2012). The concept uses the fun and addictive part of games to increase the engagement and motivation of people to achieve specific tasks through optimising status and achievements. Robinson and Bellotti (2013), Heckhausen and Heckhausen (2008).

In this chapter, we focus on gamification that uses the elements taken from video games in the design of non-gaming platforms, in order to increase public services outcome and their stakeholders' engagement.

Gamification has also been conceptualised as a process of enhancing users' value creation through the employment of affordances for a gameful experience (Huotari & Hamari, 2016). The definition of gamification proposed by Deterding et al. (2013) emphasises the core role of game elements as the design–base of gamification, however; there is no agreement in the literature on a defined set of game elements to be used in gamification. Deterding et al. (2011) themselves raised the same concern when defining gamification, suggesting limiting gamification to the use of "characteristic game elements".

4.2.2 Gamification in the Public Sector

Chin (2016) mentioned how the Taiwanese government improved the commitment of the citizens towards taxation through setting invoice numbers that motivate the consumers to demand official receipts. In the Singaporean Changi airport, the virtual reality is used to train the emergency officers on the different designed rescue scenarios. Velten (2017), Deci and Ryan (1985).

The work of Chin about how gamification is used in Salem town in Massachusetts to gather feedback about the low-income Latino neighbourhoods, shows the critical role that gamification could play in create socio-economic stability and improve public sector delivery. This gamification helped the Salem town mayor to overcome the language barrier while gathering the data from the Latino residents. Another application for overcoming languages barrier was used in Indonesia in Jakarta where the games used to communicate with the locals in their dialects to get them acquainted with the digital services.

Velten (2017) believes that the effective utilisation of gamification can create agile and efficient public sector. As per Chin (2016), there are four ways that gamification could be utilised with to improve service delivery, and better stakeholders' behaviours.

Most repeated gamification approaches focus on points, or badges or sense of winning which users earn a sense of achievement based on actions they perform, or achievements received after accomplishing an objective. The other gamification approaches also use the technique of leader-boards, which focus on the ranking of the stakeholders based on their achievements.

The characteristics of the game elements targets to create a lasting effect on the stakeholders' behaviour, motivation and make them appreciate the value creation. This lead to a focus on identifying the purpose of behavioural change. Heckhausen and Heckhausen (2008), Deci and Ryan (1985).

Gamification has great approaches that can become an innovative part of our outreach tool kit for a social or behavioural change. Using games and gamification techniques can offer non-profits and public agencies a unique and engaging way to interact with their community to promote change that benefits the individual and society. Rughiniş (2013).

Gamification is becoming more of a scientific approach to social development and change, while it started to influence many decision-makers and have its practical use in socio-economic issues. Gamification is about applying game-based thinking to organisation business, processes or new concepts or brands,

Madrid and Hunter (2012). Through gamification, we create a new experience about the inherent powers within, including the level of focus, observation and persistence. Ryan and Deci (2000).

One of the early implementations of gamification is setting different regulations for parking in the cities, which helped to regulate traffic. For example, since the early 1980s, a study in Washington DC found that the availability of free parking is associated with a 97% chance that people would drive to work alone. Gamification helped to set scoring points for the parking and create a type of competition between them. Free parking is scored as everybody takes their car; pay-for-parking is score as people start shifting to public transport depending on price. Even competition for parking spaces plays a significant role in whether you take your car into the city or use public transportation.

Another gamification in gamifying the public sector was transportation analogy. This project was applied first in Copenhagen by providing incentives by raising the availability of bike lanes and high price for parking. The rewards of biking – even in bad weather – were so superior to the high prices for parking. School grades have been a form of gamification in education which followed point scoring, competition with others and rules of play. Gamification makes the public sector more fun and impactful through engaging and involving citizens. Deterding et al. (2013).

4.2.3 Using Gamification as a Continual Improvement

Since the application of gamification is comprehensive, this chapter focuses on the non-digital realisations in public services, focusing on typical indicators and constructs used in gamification. For example, the constructs create codification, i.e. like colour coding that points to the accumulated activities within the gamification environment. The codification is similar to badges in games which are visual representations of achievements, which can be collected within the gamification environment. Rughiniș (2013), McGonigal (2011).

Visual management is used to resemble the leaderboards in games where the players are listed and usually are ranked by their success. Codification of status of achievement also represents the progress bars are used to provide information about the current status of a player towards a goal. The 'hit rate' is used to resemble performance graphs and to provide information about a players' performance, compared to past performance. McGonigal (2011).

Gamification as per Buheji (2017) is very attractive to human mindset, since it is based on incremental, achievable yet challenging goals, that are tracked by points and personal progress analysis. The gamification also uses 'quests of little tasks' where the stakeholders or the players need to fulfil to sustain a specific task, Lander et al. (2015). The gamification design needs to reflect meaningful stories. Robinson and Bellotti (2013), Deterding et al. (2011).

The idea of gamification helps to build self-determination, which creates psychological needs for competence, autonomy, and social relatedness, Sailer et al. (2013). The fulfilment of these needs fosters intrinsic inspiration, which helps people to execute challenging yet exciting service development nature. This helps to effectively and interactively to execute the task that integrates with the targeted needs. Gamification helps to define a way of penalising those who choose to do something poorly. Buheji and Ahmed (2018), Buheji and Ahmed (2017), Ryan and Deci (2000).

The mechanisms of motivations make the stakeholders more engaged with continual improvement activities until the goals are achieved. The stakeholders keep engaged and motivated to discover through experiential learning, Hense and Mandl (2012). This learning creates emotions that interact with the cognitive and motivational processes and can be influenced by instructional strategies. The stakeholders are likely to be motivated if gamification decreases negative feelings like fear, envy, and anger. Heckhausen and Heckhausen (2008), Deci and Ryan (1985).

Gamification approaches assume that people would resist extreme changes, thus they need gradual changes through approaches that make them feel rewarded or have their behaviours smoothly calibrated. Therefore, combining gamification with the process of change in the different service sectors helps to develop key performance indicators (KPIs), which in turn help us to monitor the small steps of change without resistance.

The KPIs in the gamification approaches design represent the milestones of change targeted or the values to be achieved. The approaches of gamification helps to instruct the stakeholders on how to progress and achieve their goals with few resources. The game mechanisms used in the approaches also help to define the points, the level of progression and the challenges.

The other benefit of the KPIs is that they provide immediate feedback about the extent of improvement achievement. The game mechanics such as leaderboards, progress bars, public celebrations and feels of rewards or trophies; gives a visualisation of the greatness of the achievement targeted.

4.2.4 Engagement of Stakeholders in Public Services.

Creating an environment of engagement for stakeholders with gamification approaches provide a platform for interaction and collaboration amongst themselves, through which they can positively impact their community, Alder and Goggin (2005). The stakeholders might be the process owners of the sector targeted, or the mediators, or the beneficiaries'.

The engagement used in the gamification approaches lead to knowledge development, opinion expression, common problem solving, and influence governmental decision-making. Hasan (2016) even suggested a framework for gamification of civic engagement platforms.

When the stakeholders get engaged, the proper allocation of public resources could be directed to the well-being of the community. This creates active participation of the stakeholders and makes them eager to manage a change that shapes the lives of their communities (Adler & Goggin, 2005; Rothschild, 2016). With active stakeholders' engagement, public services authorities can improve their planning, reduce costs, and increase the trust in them. Hence, reliable, competitive governments tend to foster such public involvement by innovative approaches as gamification. Chin (2016), Coronado and Vasquez (2014).

Gamification is one of the most essential tools today in changing the mindset of the stakeholders and setting effective strategies for social transformation. Through gamification, we can recognise the level of learning and achievement in the public sector, with relatively informal and immediate feedback in relevance to day-to-day practice. Besides, for the specific public sector, the gamification approaches are found to be particularly more useful to attract non-formal change. Hense and Mandl (2012).

In a nutshell, the literature still has a gap on how gamification can influence the public services through enhancing the stakeholders' engagement, Coronado and Vasquez (2014). Moreover, there is a lack of theoretical or practical frameworks as guidelines for engagement through gamification platforms. Alder and Goggin (2005).

4.2.5 Gamification Approaches and Process Motivation

Since gamification helps to maintain communities that are willing to actively engage the public participation, it creates a directional expression of motivation, Rigby (2015). The use of motivational approaches in gamification design focus on creating attention that raises both the intrinsic and extrinsic motivation of the service providers and the beneficiaries. Deterding (2012).

Gamifying a process raises the intrinsic motivation and trigger the behaviour of the internal reward system in the brain, Deci and Ryan (1985). Through gamification approaches, we can create a type of stimulation which require only limited mental efforts. Reward-based gamification is effective for quick, short-termed behavioural change that lasts for as long as the rewards are available, Rigby (2015).

Once gamification design is employed, intrinsic psychological rewards would trigger behavioural outcomes, Sailer et al. (2013). Researchers now confirm that gamification gives a feeling of process autonomy; and feeling of a community of common purpose and relatedness which enhance the stakeholders sustained engagement, Rigby (2015), Deterding (2012), Zhang (2008).

Rigby (2015) even sees that the influence of gamification in continuous improvement can be seen clearly in the changes of the individual perceptions and personalities. With gamification, we can attract all the type of specialities and personalities of stakeholders since everyone wants to be part of the achievers. Therefore, continual improvement can be achieved through bring people together and make them value accomplishments, and the common purpose. This creates a value autonomy and eases the interactions that are required for overcoming any barriers.

4.2.6 Gamification and Inspiration Labs

Gamification is based on iteration and emotion. Before we gamify any business, we need first to understand it, observe the opportunities built in it, reflect our point of view, ideate about, prototype about and do playtesting. This precisely what 'inspiration labs' do for re-inventing any business model. Inspiration labs which is one the techniques of the International Inspiration Economy Project (IIEP) helps to analyse the requirements of change, do research analysis, then establish a type of gamification frameworks, establish interdisciplinary teams, build rapid prototyping and experience playtesting. Buheji (2018), Buheji and Ahmed (2017), Robinson and Bellotti (2013), Werbach and Hunter (2012).

Buheji (2018) showed how inspiration labs techniques could solve any complex socio-economic community problems or challenges in the public sector through the method of observation. Observation target to either find opportunities inside the problem or simplify the transformation by raising the capacity to realise the change in the specific community targeted. Inspiration labs use similar elements of gamification approaches as goals, rules conflict, competition, cooperation, time, reward structures, feedback, levels, storytelling and motivation of interests. Buheji and Ahmed (2017), Kapp (2012), McGonigal (2011).

Three indicators bring together gamification and inspirational labs designs together. These key factors are mainly working to ensure the following leading indicators achieved: mechanical indicators, reward indicators, behaviour indicators and measurement indicators. Sailer et al. (2013), Deci and Ryan (1985). These indicators of gamification are influenced by behavioural game mechanics called in chapter 'gamification approaches'. The gamification Approaches are solely focused on human behaviour and can be in the form: feedback loops, progression, engagement loops, engagement and re-engagement optimisation, Alder and Goggin (2005). Thus these gamification approaches can be like: achievements badges, levels, leaderboards, progress bars, activity feeds, avatars (i.e. ideas for example), real-time feedback, challenges and quests, trophy case and mini-games within other activities. The gamification approaches help to build the gamification construct indicators, be it: mechanical-, rewards-, measurement- and behaviour-based. Hense and Mandl (2012).

The mechanical indicator in the inspiration lab and gamification focus on using storytelling, speed of responses, reward schedules, disincentives, access and social feedback. While the rewards indicator focuses on approaches as recognition, status, accessibility, the third indicator is the rewards indicator which uses approaches as the reputation, the performance, the quality, the completion, the quantity and time. The last indicator used is the behavioural indicator, which focuses on the loyalty, mastery, quality and engagement. Coronado and Vasquez (2014).

4.3 Methodology

The central goal of gamification is to capture the attention of the stakeholders and get them engaged in improving the targeted services or products. In order to support the public services, sustainable improvement, gamification approaches were proposed to influence change on a specific issue of ten selected public sectors. A table would seek to combine elements of gamification that are used in each sector management of change into then see the repeated trend that helps to build the framework.

Based on the synthesis of the literature reviewed, also the specific constructs of gamification approaches suitable for the public services are extracted. These approaches were extracted as part of problem-solving opportunities that were used in the inspiration labs, as published by the author, Buheji (2019a) and Buheji (2018). A review of the type of gamification approaches that helped to re-invent the public services activities are presented and discussed. The findings focus on the suitability of gamifying such services on the continual improvement efforts. Then, a discussion and conclusion are drawn based on the finding. Madrid and Hunter (2012), Werbach and Hunter (2012).

4.4 Case Study

4.4.1 Background about the Situation of the Public Sectors Selected in this case study

During 8/2008 till the end of 2018, there were more than 60 projects that started in the public services in the Kingdom of Bahrain through what is called 'Inspiration Labs'. These labs targeted to re-invent the way public services are delivered through the engagement of the stakeholders and with minimal resources, Buheji (2018).

For this study, we select the influence of the gamification approaches used in the 'inspiration labs' on the following ten sectors: education, water utility services, labour fund, woman affairs, traffic management, sewage sanitary services sector, police services sector and justice with legal affairs.

4.4.2 Type of Gamification Approaches

Table (1) links all the different public services sectors to the gamification approaches and stakeholders engaged.

Table (1) Gamification Approaches used in the different Public Services Activities

Sequence of Gamification Activities Used in the Inspiration Labs Projects as per the Sector Situation	Gamification Approaches	Stakeholders Engaged
One- Education Sector **Situation:** The university does not have hands-on projects and contracts that help students to practice lifelong learning skills and be more ready for the labour market. The students' get delayed in graduation in time and create more cost on the government with no effective academic advisory services due to many reasons, but the most critical is the none availability of suitable sessions to register.		

Sequence of Gamification Activities Used in the Inspiration Labs Projects as per the Sector Situation	Gamification Approaches	Stakeholders Engaged
Steps of Gamification: 1- Students were codified and classified based on fitness for graduation on time and with sufficient practical experience from University projects which address the reality of the labour market.	Codification, Performance Hit-Rate, Speed of Response, Accessibility, Quality of Engagement	Students/ Professors/ Colleges Deans Offices
2- Create competition between Colleges for attracting and then opening hands-on-projects and contracts that help students to practice lifelong-learning skills and be more ready for the labour market.	Reward scheduling Quantity and time	Professors/ Colleges Deans Offices /Potential projects partners
3- The academic advisory services are evaluated based on their capacity of graduating students' on time (within four years), and measure of the turnover of the government-subsidised chair.	Speed Batches Calibration Codification Alertness Error-Proofing	Academic advisory services/ Colleges/ Student
4- Colleges are evaluated through a program using 'smart registration' that enhances the students' choices and eliminate waste in opening extra sessions.	Leader-boards Levels Interactions Response Alertness Interactions Activity Feeds	Registration Office/ Colleges/ Students

Two- Healthcare Sector

Situation:
Bahrain and other GCC Arab Countries are considered one of the highest countries that have risks of epidemic Non-Communicable Diseases (NCD's), i.e. Diabetes, Blood Pressure, Cholesterol and Obesity. i.e. More than 80% of the population are on the WHO risk matrix scale for getting NCD during their life. On average more than 35 patients die annually in the health-centres due to heart attacks due to NCDs complications while waiting to enter to physicians in health-centres. The other major issue in Bahrain is the delay of

'Behavioural Economics'

Sequence of Gamification Activities Used in the Inspiration Labs Projects as per the Sector Situation	Gamification Approaches	Stakeholders Engaged
admission in the major general hospital in a country where emergency cases have to wait up to 72 hours before being admitted. The third main issue is the spread of poisonous disease from fast food during summer. The last but not least problem in Bahrain was the increase to suicidal rate compared to previous years.		
Steps of Gamification: **a) Gamification to deal with the High NCDs**		
a-1 Family Physicians, Health-centres, School Health Department were all trained and prepared for the competition of catchment of Non-Communicable Diseases (NCD's) Patients or those prone to get NCDs in their life. The challenge was to identify those on WHO NCD risk matrix regardless of their age. Healthcare staff were measured for their ability to meet 80% 'Hit-Rate' or more.	Challenges and Quests, Access and social feedback, Mastery	Family Physicians/ Health-centres staff/ School Health staff/ Patients /Patients families
a-2 Families Physicians are measured on their performance of counselling risk-prone families.	Quantity and Time	Family Physicians/ Health-centres staff/ /NCDs Patients families
a-3 Patients arriving health-centres do Self-Triage and codify themselves according to their level of emergency.	Mini-games	Walk-in Patients to Healthcentre
a-4 Physicians codify Psycho-Sematic Patients.	Real-time feedback	a4&a5 Family Physicians/ Patients/ Health-centres staff
a-5 Increase the Readiness of the Health centres for Emergency Cases.	Levels Progress bars	Social Workers, Health Educational Specialist and Health visitors
a-6 Competition for Optimising the role of Social Workers, Health Educational Specialist and Health visitors in family screening.	Trophy Case, Challenges and Quests, Real-time Feedback	Healthcentre Nurses Educational Institutions

87

Sequence of Gamification Activities Used in the Inspiration Labs Projects as per the Sector Situation	Gamification Approaches	Stakeholders Engaged
a-7 Classifying the type of patients' time spent with physicians as per NCDs Risk Matrix.	a-7&a-8 Activity feeds, real-time feedback, challenges and quests	Family Physicians/ Health-centres staff
a-8 Stream-mapping healthy practices in Educational Institutions towards 'NCD free Generations'.		Accident & Emergency Staff/ Wards Nurses/ Medical Consultants
a-9 Gauging the Development of the capacity to analyse the Family Profile Competition between Health Centres.	Achievements badges, levels, leaderboards, progress bars, activity feeds, time feedback, challenges	
b) Gamification to deal with Low Availability of Emergency Beds		Wards Nurses/ Medical Consultants
b-1 Stratifying the total throughput in Accident & Emergency and speed of admissions through focusing on bed turnover ratio in most congested Hospital Wards (as medical wards) and setting discharge and priority or beds based on Urgency of the cases.	b-1&b-2 Achievements badges, levels, Leaderboards, Progress bars, activity feeds, Avatars (i.e. ideas for example), real-time feedback, challenges and quests.	Wards Nurses/ Medical Consultants
b-2 Codifying the Capacity of managing the availability of the Capacity of Beds Utilisation by inspiring towards higher discharges on time and based on defined protocols & follow-up services.		
b-3 Gauge the 'Peers Review Practice' between medical consultants for Complex Cases utilising Bed for longer than five days.	b-3&b-4 Achievements badges, levels, leaderboards, progress bars, activity feeds, avatars (i.e. ideas for example), real-time feedback, challenges and quests.	Accident & Emergency Staff/ Wards Nurses/ Medical Consultants
b-5 Gauging the capacity of delivering patients home or delivering his discharge drugs on time, year-round.		Porters/ Pharmacy/Wards Nurses

'Behavioural Economics'

Sequence of Gamification Activities Used in the Inspiration Labs Projects as per the Sector Situation	Gamification Approaches	Stakeholders Engaged
c) Gamification to deal with Fast-Food Poisonous Diseases during Summer		
c-1 Codifying the 'Intelligent Inspection' that minimise the rate of poisonous calls, or low hygiene fines by 90% with less manpower and more trust worthiness enhancement.	c-1, c-2 & c-3 Achievements badges, levels, leaderboards, progress bars, activity feeds, avatars, real-time feedback, challenges and quests, trophy case and mini-games	Food Inspectors /Fast-Food Restaurants/ Consumers
c-2 Codify the reputation of fast food services that supports local tourism.		Food Inspectors /Fast-Food Restaurants/ Consumers
c-3 Codify level of intelligence of the inspection based on the outcome of hospitality services and with minimal resources.		Food Inspectors /Fast-Food Restaurants/ Consumers
d) Gamification to deal with the High Suicide		
d-1 Gauge the capacity to manage the anxiety to avoid reaching the level of chronic anxiety.	d-1 & d-2 achievements badges, levels, leaderboards, progress bars, activity feeds, avatars, real-time feedback, challenges and quests, trophy case and mini-games	d-1 & d-2 Psychiatric Clinic Staff/ Family Physicians/ Quality of Life Departments/ Public Patients /Educational Institutions
d-2 Gauge suicide ratio due to early treatment of main causalities among youth, including focusing on patients' with extended sick leave, and those with psycho-sematic symptoms.		
Three- Water Utility Services Sector **Situation:** Huge Sweat Water loss to hidden leakages that are discovered late.		

Sequence of Gamification Activities Used in the Inspiration Labs Projects as per the Sector Situation	Gamification Approaches	Stakeholders Engaged
Steps of Gamification: 1- Rewarding Inspectors and Water Authority Call Centers on their ability to intelligently forecast and detect water loss through early observation of the leakages. 2- Score the level of re-engineering in the Water Network System' Intensive Maintenance Programs and level of water-pipes Innovation and development. 3- Reward consumers in their collaboration to detect 'water loss' on time or even before time.	Challenges and Quests Mastery (4) Mini-games within other activities (i.e. within the different departments) Access and social feedback Real-time feedback Levels Progress bars Trophy Case Challenges and Quests Real-time Feedback	Water Utility Inspectors / Water Engineers/ Household Consumers Water Utility Inspectors / Water Network Engineers/ Water Pipes Companies/ Household Consumers Water Utility Inspectors / Water Authority Consumers Department/ Companies/ Household Consumers

Four- Labor Fund Sector

Situation:
Labor Fund (LF) disburse millions of dollars per years as the national fund for thousands of entrepreneurial projects and startups. However, LF in many countries and not only in Bahrain have a significant waste, and their hit-rate is below 30% of return on capital employed if we see its realised benefit in the quality of life of the middle class or the GDP. The capacity for a start-up survival is on average less than 4.5 years, despite the variety of programs pumped by the LF initiative.

Steps of Gamification: 1- Codifying and rewarding the funded projects had made a success story and build an early intervention system for the defaulters.	Avatars (the idea of pre-funding pensioners instead of just paying salary later	LF Consultants/ LF Beneficiaries/

'Behavioural Economics'

Sequence of Gamification Activities Used in the Inspiration Labs Projects as per the Sector Situation	Gamification Approaches	Stakeholders Engaged
2- Develop the capacity of start-ups since the bitching time with the development of safe exits methodology, especially for youth projects.	Trophy case (Best Start-up)	LF Consultants/ LF Beneficiaries/
3- Minimise enterprises' dependency on government purchasing.	Achievements/ badges for the level of Independence	LF Consultants/ LF Beneficiaries/ Ministry of Labour /Educational Institutes
4- Divert more mentorship on 'Necessity and Neighborhoods Entrepreneurship' to minimise low-profit margins and help for the survival of low-income families community.	Reputation & Performance Levels of Progress bars	LF Consultants/ LF Beneficiaries/ Ministry of Labour /Educational Institutes

Five- Woman Affairs Sector

Situation:
Women empowerment programs are spreading all over the world. The support of public authorities for empowering women is very clear in Bahrain as well as developing countries. However, empowerment programs do not necessarily lead to women development, which leads to country development through eco-economy and family stability.

Steps of Gamification:

1- Setup a comprehensive outcome and legacy driven national plan that changes the way woman are empowered in Bahrain by giving her more accountability to create social cohesion, stability and national competitiveness.	Achievements badges/ storytelling / Performance	Women Council/ Government/ Departments of Social Developt./ Women Leaders
2- Closing the gap and accelerating the transformation towards 'Women Development' instead of 'Women Empowerment' after 5 years from the National Plan Kick-off.	Quantity and time / Reward Scheduling	Women Empowerment NGOs & Cells

Sequence of Gamification Activities Used in the Inspiration Labs Projects as per the Sector Situation	Gamification Approaches	Stakeholders Engaged
3- Ensure knowledge sharing between Business Women, Women Entrepreneurs and Women of Productive Families Programs and especially those of the same or relevant business and link it to gamification rating. (i.e. Rating of Entrepreneurs who contribute and share knowledge)	Achievements badges, leaderboards, activity feeds, Avatars, real-time feedback, challenges and quests and mini-games	Women Entrepreneurs and Women of Productive Families

Six- Traffic Management Sector

Situation:
Despite the fact that the quality of roads designs in Bahrain and Arab GCC countries are considered to be one of the best in the world, these countries have a rising fetal accident per population. The number of black spots is increasing despite the many regulations and radar speed cameras, as the black spots areas means the areas with repeated fetal accidents.

1- Enhancing the design of the road to count for worst cases risks of accidents, due to driver, road or vehicle.	Real-time feedback	Works Dept. Road Engineers/ Traffic Police/ Municipalities
2- Scoring the speed of repair and active learning on the 'black spots' areas.	Challenges and quests	Works Dept. Road Engineers/ Traffic Police
3- Scoring Municipalities care for designing better smooth entries for junctions roads from highways.	Activity Feeds	Works Dept. Road Engineers/ Traffic Police/ Municipalities

Seven- Sewage Sanitary Services Sector

Situation:
Sewage network is one of the most expensive public services, despite not been appreciated by consumers. Annually many areas in developing countries as Bahrain suffer from sewage system blockage due to bad management by consumers.

'Behavioural Economics'

Sequence of Gamification Activities Used in the Inspiration Labs Projects as per the Sector Situation	Gamification Approaches	Stakeholders Engaged
Steps of Gamification: 1- Defining areas where sewage - drainage system designs need to be developed due to repeated blockages in the sanitary system. 2- Score the station pumps designs that need to be aligned from the time the excavation work with water and electricity authorities. 3- Evaluating and grading the sewage contractors based on results of their performance, i.e. building and maintain pumps without blockages. 4- Scoring consumers' habits and practices in dealing with sewage system and what goes into the drainage system vs what goes on waste separators. 5- Preventing solid waste or debris from going into the sewage system through a transparent program than enhances the awareness about sewage water system utilisation.	1, 2 & 3 Hit-Rate, Achievements badges, progress bars, activity feeds 4 & 5 Hit-Rate, Achievements badges, levels, leaderboards, progress bars, activity feeds, real-time feedback	Sewage System Inspectors & Engineers/ Call Centres Team Sewage System Inspectors & Engineers/ Contractors Sewage System Inspectors & Engineers/ Call Centres Team/ Consumers 4&5 Sewage System Inspectors & Engineers/ Call Centres Team/ Resturant Owners / Hair Saloons

Eight- Social Insurance

Situation:
Despite the National Social Insurance (NSI) program in Bahrain is considered to be one of the best systems, many pensioners end-up with low quality of life and limitation of resources.

Sequence of Gamification Activities Used in the Inspiration Labs Projects as per the Sector Situation	Gamification Approaches	Stakeholders Engaged
Steps of Gamification: 1- Creating a selective thinking in the way of investment of pension fund that would enhance the productivity of the national economy. 2- Scoring the reliability of the social responsibility plans towards low-income pensioner jobs are more prepared for entrepreneurship after retirement. 3- Evaluating amount of projects taken towards pensioners' 'quality of life'.	1, 2 & 3 Achievements badges, levels, leaderboards, progress bars, activity feeds, Trophy cases	NSI and Pension Fund Consultants NSI and Pension Fund Consultants / Low income pensioners NSI and Pension Fund Consultants /Low-income pensioner
Nine- Police Services Sector **Situation:** Police services do not count for security, but the safety and the harmony of the public. In Arab countries and Bahrain is no exception; there is no appreciation for prevention policing services.		

Steps of Gamification:
 	
1- Codification and Classification of the black spots in the country in relevance to:
    a. Drugs trafficking information
    b. Risk of Fire or gas leakage
    c. Jewellery theft
 	
2- Measure the prevention policing role in 'social harmony' between neighbourhood.
	1, 2, 3, 4 & 5
	Storytelling, visual cues, Response objects, reward schedules, disincentives access and social feedback recognition status access and stuff reputation performance
		Drug Assessment Specialist/ Police Drug & Narcotics Unit/ Community Policing/ Civil Defense/ Citizens
		
		Community Policing/ Social Development Dept. / NGOs

'Behavioural Economics'

Sequence of Gamification Activities Used in the Inspiration Labs Projects as per the Sector Situation	Gamification Approaches	Stakeholders Engaged
3- Reduction of transfer of cases to legal courts due to prevention policing role in creating resolutions or mediations between the families and the disputing parties in the police station.		Community Policing/ Social Development Dept. / NGOs/ Citizens
4- Enhancing Community-based Prevention Policing through improved screening and security assessment (in police stations).		Community Policing/ Social Development Dept. / NGOs / Citizens
5- Strengthening the social role of the police (the relationship between police stations and community centres).		Community Policing/ NGOs Police Stations/ Citizens
6- Raising learning and knowledge management in (Economic Crimes).	6,7,8,9,10,11&12 Hit-Rate, Achievements badges, levels, leaderboards, progress bars, activity feeds, avatars, real-time feedback, challenges and quests, trophy case and mini-games	6,7, 8 & 9 Community Policing/ Economic Crime Unit/ Social Development Dept. / NGOs/ Citizens/ Police Patrols/ Guarding Police
7- Increase the efficiency of patrols (abandoned houses)		
8- Raising efficiency and readiness (cadres guard)		
9- Enhancing community prevention through improved screening and security assessment (theft of gold shops).		
10- Reducing the criminal risk resulting from unregularly employed expats.		Community Policing/ Ministry of Labor/ Shops Owners
11- Improve the follow-up service of the communication with the stakeholder in police stations.		Community Policing
		Civil Defense / Building Owners

Sequence of Gamification Activities Used in the Inspiration Labs Projects as per the Sector Situation	Gamification Approaches	Stakeholders Engaged
12-Rasing Safety Readiness and Evacuation of residential and commercial buildings (Civil Defense). 13-Raising efficiency in gathering inferences in the Police centres in order to reduce court rejection or persecutor is returning the cases due to insufficient evidence.		Police Centre Officers / Citizens
Ten- Justice & Legal Affairs Sector **Situation:** Similar to many countries, people in Bahrain are losing confidence in the legal and justice system.		
Steps of Gamification: 1-Reduce the timings of the Legal Courts per case and avoid unjustifiable delays 2-Enhance the rights of the family in speeding up the courts' delays. 3-Establish 'resilience courts practices' in Universities where lawyers from different religious and loyalty background defend for the same case. (Legal Clinic in Law Schools)	1, 2, & 3 Hit-Rate, Achievements badges, progress bars, activity feeds, real-time feedback	1&2 Legal Courts Management Team/ Judges / Lawyers University / Legal Courts Management / College of Law

4.5 Findings

The majority of the steps of the gamification approaches were designed based on the situation of the observed and then specified public sector challenges. In general, all the gamification approaches needed some motivational engagement using rewards and behavioural constructs more than measurement and mechanical constructs. These rewards were linked to the speed of the service and using a simulation of achievement using score and batches. The challenges helped to develop the quests for the gamification approaches that lead to improvement.

Real-time feedback and levels for overcoming the challenges were identified through the codification and the classification which helped to develop the alertness and error-proofing. This also helped to develop a simulation like leader-boards that reflect levels of engagement, interactions and response to the stakeholders' issues.

The measurement constructs used in the inspiration labs that led to re-inventing the public services, came as a result of the following gamification approaches in relevance to the different activities developed: leader-boards, levels, interactions, establishing avatars, activity feeds, challenges and quests, achievements badges and progress bars.

The mechanical construct is the collective effort of the gamification approaches that are repeatedly were used in the different public services sectors. I.e. in order to achieve the desired goals that lead to re-inventing the way the public services are delivered, approaches as: hit-rate, codification, response alertness, progress bars, challenges and quests, were applied. Also, real-time feedback, avatars (i.e. as the idea of training instead of inspecting), trophy case (i.e. competition for best training), achievements badges and real-time feedback, i.e. through self-assessment anxiety forms; were used as part of the mechanical constructs gamification approaches.

Table (1) shows the sequence of gamification activities like a sequenced story that can be easily understood as a means for management of change towards the targeted improvement. This shows the importance of gamification as a technique for continual improvement, even in complicated sectors like public services.

4.6 Discussion and Conclusion

Describing a public service challenge ease its gamification that leads to developing its level of engagement with the stakeholders'. However, in for this engagement would lead to continual improvement of sectors as the public service, one need to be selective in the gamification approaches chosen.

This chapter fills a gap for the body of knowledge as it addresses the role of gamification approaches as a continuous improvement methodology. Applying gamification in special business processes, as in public sectors, helps to soften and enhance management of change. With gamification, we can engage the stakeholders in the modification of their business processes using gaming dynamics and mechanisms; without making them fear failure.

The experience of the inspiration labs run by this longitudinal project for four years could be generalised only if a theoretical framework is proposed. Therefore, using the literature review and cases in Table (1) the following framework is proposed to show how gamification could differentiate and re-invent the public services efficacy. The framework shown in Figure (1) focus on how public services could involve the stakeholders and the beneficiaries in the developing and continually improving the services, until they are re-invented or re-engineered. This can be achieved through gamification approaches that lead to improvement, based on real-time feedback.

Figure (1) propose a framework of Gamification Approaches that lead to re-Inventing Public Services

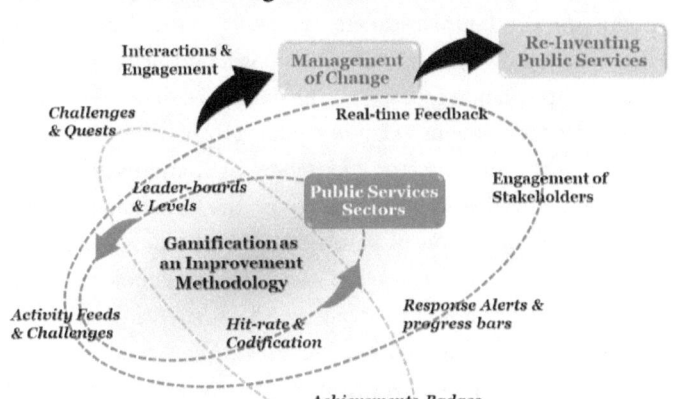

The gamification used in inspiration labs during the four years' projects in the Kingdom of Bahrain shows that there could be many innovative possibilities for public services improvement. The gamification used in this work is highly essential for re-evaluating the government services and the different possibilities for its improvement.

The indirect rewards built as part of the labs and projects approaches helped to engage the stakeholders of the different service. This could help to overcome the challenges of change that ways services are delivered. The different gamification approaches helped avoid the mixed signals about the focus of change and improved the possibility of finding opportunities inside each of the problems in the inspiration labs.

The gamification constructs help to make almost all the interventions psychologically acceptable. The mechanical and measurement constructs gamified 76% of the services. Rewards construct constitute 10% of the gamified public services, while the behavioural construct constituted 14% of the total inspiration labs carried in the different public sectors.

In the context of this chapter, we excluded gamification based on games and based on serious games. The chapter is highly suitable for think-tanks leaders, policymakers and academics. The chapter shows that gamification has its influence on many sectors, despite being focused on the public sector.

Gamification seems to ignite the capacity of different sectors, specifically the public sector, to remodel itself and to offer more adaptability and flexibility for engaging the stakeholders of the service. The simulation of gamification based projects in this study shows that involving the concerned stakeholder would bring-in appropriate dynamic partnerships between the public sector and other potential beneficiaries, thus would shift the public service policymakers from a scarcity to an abundance mindset that see the opportunities in the different exploited resources. The critical performance outcome here would is that more gamification in the plenty of public services sectors would make governmental organisation and public services providers more flexible and adaptable to future foresighted requirements.

Use of gamification would help towards the gradual convergence of realistic, sustainable public services that enhance the performance of the overall services in a short time. This study calls for more research in relevance to non-electronic gamification approaches in public sector and other socio-economic services areas which would foster economies that have an innovative and entrepreneurial spirit and that meet the demands for dynamic and diverse opportunities. The drive to establishing gamification could also create more employment opportunities that are attractive to youth in the public sector, specifically.

Gamification helps us to determine the adaptive ability of the public policy and where to invest more in relevance to the business environment, the skills profile, the institutional arrangements and type of infrastructure. Thus, gamification exploits where re-engineering or restructuring are needed most in the public sector.

The main contribution of this work is that it targets to inspire the reader to take the 'gamification of the processes' more seriously and set it as part of the sectors development or change demands. The study confirms that there are 'no one size fits all' when applying gamification to different sectors as each has their particular measurement or be approached based the conditions of the targeted beneficiary, or on the context which they are applied in. The study emphasises that the search for suitable gamification approaches could be only be achieved through experimentation.

The limitations of this study are that it is being carried in one country and as part of government inspiration labs. However, the study does not undermine recommending future studies that would explore further the influence of each gamification construct or indicators on the public services or similar other critical public services as education, municipality services, transportation, electricity and water supply and even security services. Development of interaction between all the stakeholders of these public services through the gamification approaches could help to further re-invent all these quality of life-related services to the benefit of citizens and the country in general.

References

Adler, R. and Goggin, J. (2005). What do we mean by 'civic engagement'? Journal of Transformative Education, 3(3), 236-253.

Buheji, M. (2018) Re-Inventing Our Lives, A Handbook for Socio-Economic "Problem-Solving", AuthorHouse, UK.

Buheji, M and Ahmed, D (2017) Breaking the Shield- Introduction to Inspiration Engineering: Philosophy, Practices and Success Stories, Archway Publishing, USA.

Chin, C (2016) Four ways governments are using gamification, Best practices from across Asia and beyond, June Issue, Government Insider Asia. https://govinsider.asia/security/

four-ways-governments-are-using-gamification/, Accessed: 1/1/2019

Coronado, J. and Vasquez, A. (2014). Gamification: An effective mechanism to promote civic engagement and generate trust? In Proceedings of the 8th International Conference on Theory and Practice of Electronic Governance, Oct. (pp. 514-515). Guimaraes, Portugal: ACM.

Deci, E., Ryan, R. (1985) Intrinsic motivation and self-determination in human behavior, Plenum Press, New York.

Deterding, S., S., Khaled, R., Nacke, L., Dixon, D. (2013) Gamification: Toward a Definition, Proceedings of the CHI 2011, Vancouver, Interaction Design and Architecture(s) Journal - IxD&A, N.19, pp. 28-37 9.

Deterding, S., Khaled, R., Nacke, L., Dixon, D. (2011) From Game Design Elements to Gamefulness: Defining "Gamification", Proceedings of the MindTrek 2011, Tampere.

Hasan, L (2016) Governments Should Play Games: Towards a Framework for the Gamification of Civic Engagement Platforms, December, Research Article.

https://doi.org/10.1177/1046878116683581, Accessed: 1/1/2019

Hense, J. and Mandl, H (2012) Learning in or with games? Quality criteria for digital learning games from the perspectives of learning, emotion, and motivation theory, In: D.G. Sampson, J. M. Spector, D. Ifenthaler & P. Isaias (eds.), Proceedings of the IADIS International Conference on Cognition & Exploratory Learning in Digital Age, pp. 19-26.

Heckhausen, J., Heckhausen, H. (2008) Motivation and action: Cambridge University Press, Cambridge.

Kapp, K (2012) The Gamification of Learning and Instruction: Game-based Methods and Strategies for Training and Education, Pfeiffer, San Francisco.

Landers, R., Bauer, K. and Callan, R. (2015). Gamification of task performance with leaderboards: A goal setting experiment. Computers in Human Behavior.

Madrid, W and Hunter, D (2012) For the Win: How Game Thinking Can Revolutionize Your Business., Wharton Digital Press, Philadelphia.

Robinson, D. and Bellotti, V. (2013) A Preliminary Taxonomy of Gamification Elements for Varying Anticipated Commitment, Proceedings of the CHI, Paris.

Sailer, M; Hense, J, Mandl, H and Klevers, M (2013) Psychological Perspectives on Motivation through Gamification, Interaction Design and Architecture(s) Journal - IxD&A, N.19, 2013, pp. 28-37.

Velten, J (2017) Gamifying Government: A Serious Game To Make It Agile, Innovation Lab. https://innovationlab.net/gamifying-government/, Accessed: 1/1/2019

Werbach, K., & Hunter, D. (2012) For the Win: How Game Thinking Can Revolutionize Your Business. Philadelphia: Wharton Digital Press.

Public interest statement

This study target to provide an evaluation of how none-game based gamification techniques provide practical development and re-inventing insights with a specific focus on public services. Besides, the study investigates what implications does gamification of specific sectors in the government curries in it positive changes in the policies and practices. The gamification approaches used in these targets to explore new methods that create optimism and engagement for all the stakeholders, besides the persistence desire to overcome the challenges in public services. Such gamification targets to activate curios drive for the essence of the public services provided.

PART TWO

QUALITY OF LIFE INFLUENCE ON FUTURE SOCIO-ECONOMIC LIFE

CHAPTER FIVE

Nudge Theory vs. Inspiration Economy Labs- Comparing the Depth of Influence on Socio-Economics Behaviours[5]

5.1 Introduction

Traditional socio-economic policies, practices and processes and all their instruments shown in a few centuries to be enough for the development of human achievements. Nudge is a collection of ideas from one way of thinking; IE Labs is different ways of thinking using an exploration and discovery technique with visualised goals. (Kahneman, 2011).

Sugden (2009) reviewed how Thaler became known for is the concept of the "nudge," which is a small change to someone's environment that can have a significant influence on their behaviour in economic situations. Nudge as coined by Thaler

---

[5] Buheji, M (2018) Nudge Theory vs. Inspiration Economy Labs- Comparing the Depth of Influence on Socio-Economics Behaviours, American Journal of Economics; 8(3):146-154

explain how small interventions can encourage individuals to make different decisions. Nudges can, however, be manipulative, to the detriment of individuals. (Wilkinson, 2013).

The most famous example of a nudge is forcing people to "opt-out" of default options, triggers researchers as the author and those been practising complex problems solving to wonder what is wrong with the more advanced tools that made their popularity delayed when compared to Nudge. In order to understanding this dilemma, in this study specifically, we target to compare the Nudge with IE Labs. The would be carried first through reviewing the literature of the two concepts and more deeply through analysing the characteristics of both by comparing their similarities and differences.

5.2 Literature Review

5.2.1 Introduction to BE Infleunce

BE incorporates the study of psychology into the analysis of the decision-making behind an economic outcome, such as the factors leading up to a consumer buying one product instead of another. BE, along with the related sub-field behavioural finance, studies the effects of psychological, social, cognitive, and emotional factors on the economic decisions of individuals and institutions and the consequences for market prices, returns, and resource allocation. (Sunstein, 2015). Even though the field of BE became widely known through (2017) Noble prize winner Richard Thaler, there are other notable Nobel laureates as Gary Becker (motives, consumer mistakes; 1992), Herbert Simon (bounded rationality; 1978), Daniel Kahneman (illusion of validity, anchoring bias; 2002) and George Akerlof (procrastination; 2001) who had done many great work that added to the importance of this field directly and indirectly.

5.2.2 Defining Nudge Theory

The concept is a relatively subtle policy shift that encourages people to make decisions that are in their broad self-interest. Nudge as Richard Thaler and Cass Sunstein (2008) "By knowing how people think, we can make it easier for them to choose what is best for them, their families and society". It is not about penalising people financially if they do not act in certain way. It's about making it easier for them to make a particular decision. (Cambridge Dictionary, 2018; Sugden, 2009).

Over the past few decades, there have been many improvements made on the way that consumer behaviour is analysed. One of the more recent concepts on consumer behaviour is known as the nudge theory. (Hansen, 2016).

5.2.3 Defining Inspiration Economy

One of the best contemporary focused work on Inspiration was explored by Thrash and Elliot (2004) where it was defined as a state of transmission of newly appreciated qualities of a particular object based on creative ideas that would lead to a creative invention or a tangible product and/or service. Recent studies explore how inspiration approaches can effect transformations from being situational, to becoming self-driving forces that use the intrinsic powers, cognitive and non-cognitive to create a differentiated value added solutions, especially during times of challenges and failures (Buheji, 2016).

IE that focuses on raising the capacity of discovering the potential of human beings' abilities to be the currency of competition and source of a planned outcome and legacy. Thus inspiration economy is a mix of many disciplines that lead to inspiration practices that motivate the spirit to a level that creates waves of inspiration in socio-economic development.

5.2.4 Defining Management of Opportunity

Opportunity is defined as the potential insight for a better change, or improvement that come from the actions that come from the circumstances, or environment conditions faced (Hansen, 2016). Opportunities thus found be many researchers and practitioners to bring in the spirit of positivity and to offer the potential for personal development. Opportunities help to bring in both an entrepreneurial and socio-behavioural processes that depend on interaction with the surrounding environment. Thus opportunities have effectively managed an improvement to socio-economic change efforts can occur from the action. (Buheji and Ahmed, 2017a)

5.2.5 Exploiting and Monopolising the Opportunity

Both Nudge and IE work on exploiting and monopolising opportunities. Discovering and monopolising opportunities depends on cognitive abilities and interaction with new services, new products and ideas from the external environment. It also focuses on business planning before the exploitation of opportunity where risks are handled by predicting the future. (Buheji, 2018b; Ariely, 2008).

Development of linear planning and rational thinking over social factors strengthen the opportunity outcome (Shane, 2000). Once the opportunity is ready, it can be exploited and monopolised. Hisaka (2015) mentioned that opportunities are usually hidden inside three common problems. They are hidden in qualified leads, in curious, investigative research and prospects with personalised information. Most potential hidden opportunities are considered complex when it involves the public or the community change of mindset, due to the complexity of communication and the network setting. Buheji (2018b).

For IE labs, the opportunity would lead to an inspiration currency which enhances the power to inspire. Having a stable currency means that you can create influence with it, or even you can drive change through utilising it effectively (Cialdini, 1998). Cohen-bradford has set a model in (2005) that can be used for inspiration currency enhancement through focusing on the big picture (vision), excellence practices and values.

5.2.6 Psychology of Nudge and Inspiration Economy Labs

Nudge is emblematic of a series of high profile texts from mainly American authors (Ariely, 2008; Cialdini, 1998; Shiller, 2005) who explore the importance of behavioural and psychological factors in shaping social, environmental and economic decisions and outcomes. At the heart of these texts is a critique of economic theory which is based on rational assumptions; these authors argue that social and behavioural factors matter, and in particular expound arguments around the significance of a human being's bounded rationality. In making choices, humans do not have 'full attention, perfect information, unimpaired cognitive ability and complete self-control' (Sugden, 2009).

IE Labs, similar to Nudge, they come mainly from two fields Psychology and Economic. Economic theories are built usually based on addressing how humans can make decisions. However, over the last three decades, there has been significant development with relevance to positive psychology and socio-economic behaviours.

BE theories such as happiness, wellbeing and inspiration started to build standard psychological bridges with other experiential economies concepts. All these activities promote divergent thinking as they are linked to attempts of discovery. This type of attempts helps people mitigate challenges, overcome failures, break their fear of taking risks, build persistent personalities and have a strong ability to learn and adapt. Vosburg

(1998) explored how the improvement of divergent thinking helps us to move beyond the quality of ideas.

Thus, for Inspiration Labs, this type of thinking produces standardised life exams while divergent thinking uses lifelong learning practices that open up a variety of potential unseen opportunities. Lieberman (1965) mentioned five traits of such convergent thinking that can add value to inspiration model development. Convergent thinking found to be of physical, social, cognitive advantage.

5.2.7 Applications of Nudge and Inspiration Economy

According to BE, nudging is the process of influencing consumers' behaviour in predictable ways by changing the choice architecture. To be considered as a nudge, the intervention should not restrict the available options. Also, the intervention should not bring about significant change in the economic benefit to the consumer. In this article, I have attempted to cite a few examples of nudges that I have observed. (Ariely, 2008).

The UK government, followed by the USA, established nudge units to apply certain practices in the government. One of the practices was re-writing tax reminder letters using principles of BE, which it said helped to bring forward more than £200m for the government in one year. (Sanders and Halpern, 2014). Chakrabortty (2008) mentioned how David Cameron, in 2010, tried to improve public services and save money. Nudge was applied to improve the management of pension, taxes, prevention from mobile phone theft, prevention of the negative impact of e-cigarettes, unemployment, foster care, army recruitment, police diversity, adult education and charitable giving. (Instituteforgovernment.org.uk., 2010).

Administrations in Denmark, Australia, Canada and the Netherlands have also started the same Nudge units. Such programs started to emphasis greater personal responsibility in

'Behavioural Economics'

healthcare (e.g., tackling obesity), welfare (e.g., conditionality on unemployment benefit claimants), energy efficiency, household recycling and consumer credit. Chakrabortty (2008).

IE labs came from a government program that was established in Bahrain and continued for three years. The labs changed the way the government see problems and how they deal with them as opportunities (Buheji, 2017). Buheji and Ahmed (2017a) reporting how inspiration engineering and labs changed how problems and hidden opportunities are capitalised upon in basic and higher education, social development, electricity services, water services, primary care, secondary care, public health, health enrichment, psychiatric services, applied science colleges, industry sector, commercial sector, training & development, pension fund, quality assurance in education, labour fund, labour market authority, woman council, customs, visa and passport services, municipality services, research and development, minimising traffic accidents, sanitary services, social insurance, municipalities and urban development, national centre for exhibitions and conferences, roads works, tender board, housing services, police services, ports and marine services and land ownership and registration. (Buheji, 2016; Buheji and Ahmed, 2017a). Since 2015, IE labs spread in other areas in the world focusing more on civil entities services in different countries with specific experience in Bosnia and Morocco.

5.2.8 Importance of Influencing without Power Principles

Both literature of Nudge and IE labs claim to influence people or organisations or community without exerting more power on them or even utilising more resources as a means. Real influence provokes change. Influence is only valuable when it provokes change in how people operate and think; when it inspires them to take necessary action. Influence is more about reciprocity (give and take) between you and another person(s) or between organisations and communities which enables change to happen or attitudes, opinions, or behaviours to be reinforced as per Cohen and Bradford (2005).

Johnson (2008) mentioned the influence that is built on gaining access to resources needed to be carried out by outstanding efforts. For example, gaining access to resources needed with minimal investment of efforts, using more sound pieces of evidence. Johnson that influence clearly happens when doors swing open freely to those key players whose cooperation needed most. That time we will feel we have achieved central purpose while catalysing valuable change for the targeted community. Cialdini (1998).

Influencing without power found to create more impact and lasting effect in relevance to socio-economic problems as poverty, low aspirations, quality of life, youth demands, social and political instability, low productivity, business instability and issues of migrations. If we influence with minimal resources and without using any official power, people would be more committed to creating more differentiated results and outcomes compared to what is expected. Buheji (2016) mentioned about more demand being more frequent waves of innovation and with the spread of unstable coexistence or resilience, influencing without power and with minimal resources can create more differentiation for communities' outcomes.

5.2.9 Nudge and Inspiration Economy Mechanisms in Social Engineering

John et al. (2009) compare a normative political science approach of 'think think' based deliberative democracy to the economic libertarian paternalism of 'nudge nudge'. In contrast to Nudge principles based on individuals, they emphasise that decision making which takes place in groups, with discussion and deliberative action by citizens, potentially leads to better collective decisions.

'Behavioural Economics'

They emphasise that individuals do not have fixed preferences, but rather through expressing different points of view consensus may be reached. The authors point to the United Kingdom and international examples such as participatory budgeting and citizens' juries and panels. Another example would be the New Deal for Communities, whereby neighbourhood elections were used to select board members of local partnership bodies.

For Nudge "Do not Mess with Texas", social advertisement campaign would be considered as a social engineering method, as per Thaler and Sunstein (2008). In IE, this would be considered growth and not a development resource-dependent tool that uses the method of (supply vs demand) than (capacity vs demand), Buheji (2016). Even if as per Thaler and Sunstein (2008) that roadside litter was reduced by 72 %, there are no guarantees that such achievements would be maintained. The purpose of IE Labs as mentioned in (Buheji and Ahmed, 2017a) is that cultures do not change unless involvement and engagement techniques are utilised to challenge the human or community assumptions.

Nagatsu (2015) seen that "Do not mess with Texas" anti-littering campaign can work if it managed to change the expectations that others will not litter (and expect them not to litter). Mills (2015) argues that such nudge programs are compatible with the autonomy of people if it facilitates the Nudgee's pursuit own goal while having an acceptably low opt-out cost and satisfying conditions of publicity and transparency.

Lobel (2008) asserts that Nudge is usually built around every possible situation where a choice architecture might exist. Such a process would involve asking what mechanism underlies potential biases and what mechanism the potential solution might require. Lobel highlight that restructuring choices may lead to unintended consequences because individuals react adversely to having their decisions manipulated.

Through preserving the libertarian position of not infringing on individual choice, Thaler and Sunstein are thus overly concerned with ensuring that there is a near zero-cost to opt-out. A central concern for Thaler and Sunstein is that there exists sufficient information and evidence from which choices can be structured. Unfortunately, the choice is a contingent process from which individuals will not know the full outcomes at the time of decision making. From a libertarian perspective, even where an individual's choices are incoherent, they remain the property of the individual and therefore leave unclear. Hence, the goal of a nudge is to "alter people's behaviour in a predictable way" (Thaler and Sunstein 2008), to "steer people in particular directions" (Sunstein 2015). However, nudge should be "easy to avoid" and not forbid any option; as Thaler and Sunstein (2008) say: "We strive to design policies that maintain or increase freedom of choice".

Inspiration Labs are about BE where the eagerness and the psychology of discovery are based on the behavioural change that effectively inspires people to make more compassionate choices targeting social change. Life observations and reflections, as per IE labs would help people and organisation to see and visualise the big picture that to create better realisations of certain life, organisational or social challenges by turning them into opportunities. Through the practices of (Inspiration Engineering) the ability to challenge many status quo situations through disruptive thinking techniques are increased. This provides the organisation or the community with abundant opportunities for innovative ideas to follow and which usually are socially ignored or resisted. Buheji and Ahmed (2017a).

5.3 Methodology

Comparative research in social sciences aims to explore or discover the differentiation and the value-added characteristics of two issues or principles, or more. The technique used in each comparative study might often utilise multiple approaches. Øyen (2004).

The qualitative comparative study in this chapter looks for differences between the two social change approaches and then looks at these differences concerning some other variables that are expected from a "BE" concept such as level and type of behavioural change created, level of capacity development, influence on the social welfare and mindset change. A suggested modification based on the opportunities for improvement would affect the outcome for such comparison where changes would specific to enhance the utilisation of each concept in its right time and place. Øyen, (2004).

5.4 Comparative Study

5.4.1 In this comparative study, the focus was on the following main criteria's:

a) the level and type of behavioural change created,
b) level of capacity development,
c) influence on social welfare, and
d) mindset change

Thus the following comparisons were made:

Comparison 1 – Basis of Power of Each Principle

BE draws on psychology and economics to explore why people sometimes make irrational decisions, and why and how their behaviour does not follow the predictions of economic models. While IE focuses on exploring the intrinsic power within the individual through the technique of observing and discovering the opportunities, which in turn would change the mindset which the attitude and behaviour are part of it.

Comparison 2 – Way of dealing with people

Nudge about pushing people to decide a specific direction, while IE labs are about exploring unforeseen opportunities and creating a reverse thinking, or pull thinking in a particular area that would create more inspiration currency that leads to changes in assumption and then behaviours.

Nudge theory is being marketed as being particularly useful for organisations and companies looking to encouraging changes in behaviour by consumers, however, in reality, it is more of a manipulation technique that can be used for setting public policy mapping and control of people towards specific choices of services delivery. Tinkler (2011).

Comparison 3 – Way of Developing the Behavioural Change

While Nudge is developed based on studying consumer behaviour, IE labs focus on changing the consumer behaviours through finding opportunities that would help the consumers to participate in being part of the solution. The chronic problem in the society for IE labs open opportunities to discover hidden opportunities, or mitigating its probability for occurrence.

Comparison 4 – Simplicity of Solutions vs Complexity of Problem

Nudge would have made a specific protocol that leads patients to accept the prioritisation of beds availability for emergency cases. Hence while Nudge would develop a tool, i.e. to push the families or the patient to choose to leave the hospital as soon as they are on the road of recovery; IE labs would see an opportunity that this problem need totally solved through re-engineering the triage system, or the practices of the patients discharge system and its relevant protocols and practices.

Comparison 5- Role in Creating Effective Decision Making

Nudge is about enhancing "the making" or the decision making, IE sees that factual decision making is about seeing totally new solutions inside problems and challenges which are considered to be treasures of opportunities. Both principles depend on facts and analysis of primary data that would help to direct their effective plan.

Comparison 6- Level of Human Change

Nudge uses BE to seek to explain why an individual decided to go for choice A, instead of choice B. Nudge use humans ease distracted and push them to make decisions that are presumed to their self-interest. IE Labs is more than pushing towards self-interest; it focuses on creating humans with life-purposefulness by making them visualise a bigger picture. Such humans as per IE would be more competent to both create and sustain change as they become believers.

Comparison 7- Mind vs Mindset

Nudge is more of a mind manipulation technique, while IE labs work on changing the assumptions that are part of the mindset.

Comparison 8- Type Positive Re-Enforcement

Nudge theory focuses on positive re-enforcement that influence motivations and decision-making. IE is about using challenges and problem solving to help inspire the society of its hidden opportunities.

Comparison 9- Dealing with Hidden Opportunities

Hidden opportunities are opportunities that can be found inside each problem or challenge. Hidden opportunities cannot be seen due to our way of thinking and constrained mindset. Nudge work to find hidden opportunities in the processes of the service delivery from the beginning in order to use it for manipulation design of behavioural decisions. IE Labs target intentionally to enhance the process of discovering hidden opportunities gradually through the practice of observation that leads absorption and then a level of realisation that would help to overcome a complex challenge whiling setting enablers that would sustain such achievement.

Comparison 10-Ways of Influencing without Power

Nudge use influencing without power since the beginning by designing a system that influences individual decision making through manipulation without restricting the power of choice, i.e. the power to opt-out. IE labs consider influencing without power is an outcome based on the ability to change the mindset of the individual, or the organisation to pilot and explore to discover the hidden opportunities that would create the success story.

5.2 Success Stories of Nudge vs Inspiration Economy Labs

Both Nudge and IE Labs are pragmatic principles that turn the discovered opportunities into success stories. Based on an extensive review of Thaler since early 1990's published work related to Nudge and Buheji work published since 2015-2018, a comparative table was established with a specific example. However, Nudge success stories seem to be simple, and this is a point of strength and weakness in the same time; while IE Labs success stories seem to be complicated and represent a real holistic story that has ups and downs and real challenges and failures.

One observation on Nudge success stories that they are not actually made in labs, but rather it is descriptive of certain practices and achievements of others. 50% of the mentioned below Nudge stories are not published work and have been retrieved from the internet from different Nudge teams in countries as Finland, UK and USA. All the innovation of IE labs comes from its success on challenging the mindset and applying the best tools to foster new knowledge thus building long-term collaborative problem-solving capacity. We could understand this differentiation more by seeing the following examples in Table (1). The structure used in this table would be mentioning an actual IE Lab relevant to the known Nudge story in the different subjects, as both principles being multi-disciplined.

Table (1) Comparison of Nudge vs. IE Success Stories

Nudge Success Stories	IE Labs Success Stories
Private Sector employees not enrolling in the Pension Fund Auto Enrolment for Pension for Private Sector employees	Improving Social Insurance Pushing social insurance to invest in SME's as a partner to enhance the socio-economy and also elevate the trust of those on pension and non-pension to opt-in.
Encouraging Walking Decisions Putting walking steps towards the staircase, instead towards the lift	Improving Quality of Life Programs Family Physicians and Primary care staff define specially program for families with the risk of obesity, cholesterol, high blood pressure and diabetes.
People are not Saving Envelop (with their Children Photo on it)	Enhancing Central Bank (CB) Protection of People Savings and Mitigation of Level of Debts. CB investigate and calculate the risk factors for each bank and ensure its capacity to return the savings of people + ensure that banks do not further people being on debt beyond their capacity.
Huge Wasted Food Cut fruits in small pieces and cake (sweets) too, they add more fruits if smaller sizes Downsising the plates in Buffet in the restaurants & especially in hotels	Changing Food Inspection to be Food Quality Improvement Mentors. Inspectors are measured through inspiration lab to follow more mentorship and reduce food poisonous diseases through enhancing their ability to influence positive change, including enhancing management of food and improving its quality.

Nudge Success Stories	IE Labs Success Stories
Nudging Smoking Habits To more clearly show the negative effects of smoking, many countries have started to add deterrent pictures on the cigarette packages with images that display damaged organs that can be a consequence of long term smoking. This is meant to discourage people to start smoking and motivate people that are smokers to quit.	Improving Early Discovery of Lung Cancer Codification, Classification and stratification of type of smokers using gamification techniques.
Nudging towards Healthy Food Overconsumption of calorie-rich food can lead to a deteriorating health. In an attempt to get employees to eat healthier, a company rearranged its cafeteria. Healthy food was placed at eye-level and easily available for the visitors of the cafeteria. Unhealthy food, such as candy or snacks, was placed behind the counter to make them less visible and accessible for the visitors in the cafeteria. The idea with this intervention is to encourage the consumption of healthier alternatives to improve the health of the employees. Marteau et al. (2011).	Re-Engineering in Services There are lots of projects reported by Buheji (2016a), and Buheji and Ahmed (2017a) showed that one could business process re-engineering (BPR) to switch the consumers to a specific decision. BPR could be used for enhancing the empathetic engineering for Agricultural Services thus to use the farm to enhance the government-owned gardens in planting and harvesting healthy organic food while supporting the reduction of organic food prices and giving mentorship for all retail partners interested in organic farming. This study was reported in Buheji (2018a).
Organ Donations There is currently a lack of organ donors in many countries. One way to increase the number of organ donors could be to automatically enrol people as organ donors unless otherwise specified (so-called Opt-Out).	Recycling Participation People for the specific pilot area given a choice to opt-out if they do not want to participate in a waste recycling program. 90% of the local homeowners choose to stay opt-in in the program. The program brought a profit of about US$ 100,000 just in the first three months besides proven that the locals are willing to recycle the waste without the help of the government.

Nudge Success Stories	IE Labs Success Stories
Boosting Selling of Specific Products Marketing specific products to enhance consumers decisions through Nudging consumer towards "most popular selling", "that much sold", "Discounted price for a limited time", "Game Over Scores."	Boosting Selling for Camel Wool Organic Hand-Made Carpets IE Labs in a Camel Wool Carpet Factory focused on enhancing the sharing economy of a woman working in carpets by having machines set in villages rather than factory and focusing on hand-made plus organic wool value, besides innovative story-based packaging to boost sales in the factory.
Improving People honesty about car mileage for Car Insurance Change the signing of confirming honest information to be on top before starting the car millage	Improving Capitalisation of Islamic Insurance Fund (IFI). IFI found to have low-profit due non-optimisation of its funds. IE labs helped to improve the Return on Capital Employed in IFI.
Improving the Traffic flow Separating between the pedestrian and pikers by small yellow tape	Reducing Traffic Accidents while improving the Traffic Flow A review of the black sports areas (i.e. areas with repeated fatal accidents, or those with a high risk of becoming so), led to the identification of specific roads designs that need to be modified and mitigate the risks that the speed and quantity of vehicles flow. A countermeasure was taken for all these roads without first roads modification which reduced accidents by 30-40% in almost all black spots. Only 10% of the roads where re-designed.

Nudge Success Stories	IE Labs Success Stories
Abandoned Cart Problem *"Abandoned cart sales"* is one of the biggest problems faced by the e-commerce industry. An abandoned cart sale happens at the end of the customer journey: the customer visits the website to buy, adds the product to the cart but does not complete the transaction. The e-commerce industry is losing about $3 trillion USD in sales due to abandoned cart sales. The average cart abandonment rate is about 68% according to Baymard Institute. Thaler suggests changes can be made to an individual's "choice environment" to influence their behaviour to complete the transactions. The best example of this comes in the supermarket, where the attention of the consumers is drawn to specific products at the end of the supermarket to encourage them to spend more money on such products. (Sunstein and Thaler, 2003).	**Abandoned Flats in Housing Services** Many citizens in the rich Arab Gulf States abandon or refuse to receive flat instead of villas, due to level of income. This affects the country economy, space, urban planning and delays people quality of life. To reduce the gap between citizens' demands and their quality of life needs, IE labs made a significant improvement in Public Housing Service, where flats are redesigned according to youth or new couples, variety of financial and non-financial service options in non-villa packages (i.e. flats) were introduced. This managed to reduce the rising negative social inequality and improved social coexistence through post-housing services.

5.5 Discussion

There are lots of learning that can be discussed from both Nudge and IE Labs. Both principles use opportunities, however, the influence and goals in many times much difference, even though both also work in creating a major development in the community that leads to a major outcome or even a legacy.

5.5.1 Learning 1- Way of Spreading the Concept

Nudge comes from a work that exceeds twenty years by Richard Thaler and those who believed gradually on the concept of BE that Nudge summarised its peak success. In the case of IE Labs, it is a concept that started only a few years ago and it would need the time to accepted and spread in both the academic and practitioners' community, despite its power of creating more sophisticated change.

Nudge uses significant government opportunities, or major marketing opportunities to do its proposed intervention. IE Labs have been concentrating in doing labs in the field of governments and civil community where challenges are turned into opportunities through piloted exploration till problems are cracked.

5.5.2 Leaning 2- Ease of examples and application.

Nudge clearly surpass IE labs in its ease of examples. However, IE labs have shown that it has a history of cracking more complicated problems or challenges that Nudge or BE did not tackle, and it is highly relevant to socio-economy of any community or organisation.

5.5.3 Learning 3- Rational Choice vs Discovering Intrinsic Power

In economics, the rational choice theory states that when humans are presented with various options under the conditions of scarcity, they will choose the option that maximises their individual satisfaction. This theory assumes that people, given their preferences and constraints, are capable of making rational decisions by effectively weighing the costs and benefits of each option available to them. The final decision made will be the best choice for the individual. The rational person has self-control and is unmoved by emotions and external factors and, hence, knows what is best for himself. BE explains that humans are not rational and are need not always make the right decisions. Sen (2002).

The rational choice manipulation as per Nudge theory would be "opting-in" by checking a box on that was changed as a default on the form and assume that everyone signing would be an organ donor, for example, unless they opt-out and choose otherwise not to donate. For IE Labs, the issue for organ donors would be enhancing how to make people discover the benefits of organ donations to the wellbeing of the community and which they are the direct beneficiary of it. IE Labs focus on changing the mindsets instead using the manipulation of people decision.

5.5.4 Learning 4- Influence of Nudge and Inspiration Economy

Influencing the mindsets to make organisations, and communities get more engaged to create a focused outcome towards a targeted legacy (Hogg and Cooper, 2007; Mathieu et al., 2000). The level of influence is very important for inspiration based economy, as without such level of influencing people cannot see how inspiration would leave an impact on the economy and the socio-economy, (Buheji, 2016 and 2017). The work of Thaler and his colleagues also focus on influencing people; however, through diverting their decision to what is believed to be towards their own benefit.

In today busy life, we need to influence with minimal resources and the quick impact that can be felt by more people. Both concepts Nudge and IE labs use influencing without power as part of problem-solving and problem finding that lead to overcoming complexity and the creation of development.

Both concepts see that the more we influence people towards positive change, the more we own the currency to change them, or at least create in them the will to take action. However, the level of influence depends on perception and expectations as well as the spirit. In IE Labs influence can be improved with the level of visualisation which would improve the accuracy of hit rate. Both visualisation and better hit rate would enhance the direction focus and create a selective mindset that helps to discover and create new learning and thus raise the capacity vs demand. (Buheji and Ahmed, 2017a)

5.5.5 Learning 5- Social Applications of Nudges and Inspiration Economy

Nagatsu (2015) explored the use of social nudges in policy interventions that would induce voluntary cooperation in social dilemma situations which can be defended against two ethical objections that are the objections from coherence and autonomy. Thaler and Sunstein (2008) popularised libertarian paternalism, the idea that behavioural economics and psychology "the emerging science of choice" provides policymakers with new tools to influence people's economic and other choices for their own benefit without compromising their freedom of choice.

Nudges are subtle behavioural interventions that are distinct from standard regulations that operate with incentives. Although nudges have already been applied as behavioural public policy in a wide range of domains (Shafir 2013), nudge paternalism has attracted ethical and moral debate. IE labs have had many social applications in public, civil and private sector. For IE, coexistence and establishing effective social cohesion programmes can bring about more productive citizens that provide value-added to the broader community (Buheji, 2016).

The observation of the current market setting in both Nudge and IE labs leads societies to go deeper in understanding individualistic behaviour.

5.5.6 Attempts for Effective Behavioural Change

Thaler and Sunstein (2008) characterise a nudge as any aspect of the choice architecture that predictably alters people's behaviour without forbidding any options or significantly changing their economic incentives. To use the famous examples from Thaler and Sunstein (2008), it is supposed to be easy and cheap to avoid healthy food in a cafeteria, or opt-out from a contribution plan for retirement saving or choosing healthy food. Nudge seen by some as morally unacceptable as they induce behavioural changes to which one's reasoning process is not responsive.

IE not only enhance the opportunities and support based on intrinsic resources but extrinsic ones too. This creates a movement to behavioural attitudes and habits of the inter-dependence level. During inspiration, attitudes and behaviour start to be challenged due to new feelings or actions that are caused by this sense of inspirational energy. Being self-conscious, due to the nature of IE lab, will lead to people to be more able to create a stronger and more compelling change thus sharing best practices that enhances the targeted outcome.

5.6 Conclusion

This chapter set a line between Nudge and IE labs and their role in creating behavioural change outcomes. Even though it is clear from the discussion of the comparative study that Nudge have got much time for maturity and thus reflected in its popularity thanks to the huge work of Thaler and his colleagues; IE labs is clearly a coming star that would complement the work of Nudge, or even fill the gaps in significant areas for societies development.

Nudge has shown transparent, simple methodologies that lead to influencing social welfare, while IE labs have a differentiated outcome when it comes to capacity development. IE labs also shown a clear methodology in changing mindsets which partly helping to improve people decisions or government outcome.

The six learnings from the comparisons of Nudge vs IE labs shows that Nudge surpasses IE labs in the way of marketing and spreading the concept and ease of examples and applications followed. Maybe this is due to the focus of Nudge on manipulating the rational choices, instead of trying to discover the intrinsic powers within the organisation or the community. Both Nudge and IE labs show clearly that they are using influencing without power; however, the techniques and sustainability of each differ. Both concepts also managed to make social applications that lead to better effective behavioural change.

The researcher recommends more work to be continued in this line due to the richness of the data available and the need of all the socio-economics to utilise these multiple disciplined driven concepts further in more applications that lead to the improvement of communities' quality of life and in the way the human mindset is utilised.

References

Ariely, D. (2008) Predictably Irrational: The Hidden Forces that Shape Our Decisions. London: Harper Collins.

Buheji, M. (2018a) Role of Empathetic Engineering in Building More Resilient

Green Economy. Case Study on Creating Resilient Self Sufficient Food Security Programs in Middle East, Advances in Social Sciences Research Journal, 5(3) 148-157.

Buheji, M. (2018b) The Art of Capturing Opportunities— Screening Arab Social Entrepreneurs. American Journal of Industrial and Business Management, 8, pp. 803-819.

Buheji, M. (2018c) Influencing without Power" Currency in Inspiration Labs -A Case Study of Hospital Emergency Beds. American Journal of Industrial and Business Management, Vol. 8, pp. 207-220.

Buheji, M and Ahmed, D (2017a) Breaking the Shield- Introduction to Inspiration Engineering: Philosophy, Practices and Success Stories, Archway Publishing, Simon & Schuster, USA.

Buheji, M (2017) Understanding Problem-Solving in Inspiration Labs, American Journal of Industrial and Business Management, 7, pp. 771-784,

Buheji, M and Ahmed, D (2017b) Understanding the Role of 'Inspiration Productivity, International Journal of Current Advanced Research Volume 6; Issue 3; April 2017; Page No. 2866-2871, http://journalijcar.org/sites/default/files/issue-files/1679-A--2017.pdf

Buheji, M and Ahmed, D (2017c) A Holistic Review for Inspiration Economy Framework Constructs. Journal of Social Science Studies, Vol. 4, No. 1 - ISSN 2329-9150.
http://www.macrothink.org/journal/index.php/jsss/issue/view/528

Buheji, M and Ahmed, D (2016a) Application of Differential Diagnosis in Inspiration Economy Labs – A Literature Review, International Journal of Applied Business and Economic Research, 13(8), 2016: 3681-3687

Buheji, M and Ahmed, D (2016b) In Search for Inspiration Economy Currency—A Literature Review. American Journal of Industrial and Business Management, 6, 1174-1184.

Buheji, M (2016c) Handbook of Inspiration Economy. Bookboon. ISBN: 978-87-403-1318-5.

Cambridge Dictionary (2018) Meaning of Nudge,
https://dictionary.cambridge.org/dictionary/english/nudge

Chakrabortty, A (2008) From Obama to Cameron: why many politicians want a piece of Richard Thaler. The Guardian 12 July.

www.guardian.co.uk/politics/2008/jul/12/economy

Cialdini, R (1998) Influence: The Psychology of Persuasion. London: Collins.

Cohen, A., and Bradford, D. (2005). Influence Without Authority (2nd ed.). New Jersey: Wiley.

Hansen, P. (2016) The Definition of Nudge and Libertarian Paternalism: Does the Hand Fit the Glove? European Journal of Risk Regulation, 7(01), pp.18-20.

Instituteforgovernment.org.uk. (2010) MINDSPACE: Influencing behaviour through public policy. https://www.instituteforgovernment.org.uk/sites/default/files/publications/MINDSPACE.pdf, Accessed: 12/4/2018.

John, P., Smith, G. and Stoker, G. (2009) Nudge Nudge, Think Think: Two Strategies for Changing Civic Behaviour. Political Quarterly, 80, 361-370.

Kahneman, D (2011) Thinking, fast and slow. London: Macmillan.

Levitt, S. and List., J (2009) Field experiments in economics: the past, the present, and the future. European Economic Review, 53(1): 1–18.

Lobel, O. (2008), 'Stumble, Predict, Nudge: How BE Informs Law and Policy'. Columbia Law Review, 108, 2098-2138.

Osborne, G. (2008) Nudge, Nudge, win, win. The Guardian, 14 July.

Marteau, T., Ogilvie, D., Roland, M., Suhrcke, M. and Kelly, M. (2011). Judging nudging: can nudging improve population health? BMJ, 342, pp.228-d228.

Nagatsu, M (2015) Social Nudges: Their Mechanisms and Justification, Review of Philosophy and Psychology, 6 (3), 481-494.

Øyen, E. (2004) Living with imperfect comparisons, In Kennett, P. A Handbook of Comparative Social Policy. Edward Elgar. pp. 275–291.

Sanders, M., and Halpern, D (2014) Nudge unit: our quiet revolution is putting evidence at heart of government. The

Guardian. http://www.theguardian.com/public-leaders-network/small-businessblog/2014/feb/03/nudge-unit-quiet-revolution-evidence, Accessed: 12/4/2018.

Sen, A. (2002) Rationality and Freedom. Harvard: Harvard Belknap Press.

Shiller, R.J. (2005) Irrational Exuberance. New York: Princeton University Press.

Sunstein, C.R. (2015) Nudges, agency, and abstraction: a reply to critics. Review of Philosophy and Psychology, 6, pp. 511–529.

Sugden, R (2009) On Nudging: A Review of Nudge: Improving Decisions About Health, Wealth and Happiness by Richard H. Thaler and Cass R. Sunstein, International Journal of the Economics of Business, Vol 16, Issue 3, Oct, pp 365-373. https://doi.org/10.1080/13571510903227064, Accessed: 12/4/2018.

Sugden, R (2008) Why incoherent preferences do not justify paternalism. Constitutional Political Economy, 19(3), pp.226-248.

Sunstein, C and Thaler, R (2003) Libertarian Paternalism Is Not an Oxymoron. The University of Chicago Law Review, 70, 4, 1159-1202.

Sunstein, C and Thaler, R (2009) Nudge: Improving Decisions About Health, Wealth and Happiness. 1st ed.

Sugden, R (2009) Market simulation and the provision of public goods: A non-paternalistic response to anomalies in environmental evaluation. Journal of Environmental Economics and Management, 57(1), pp.87-103.Top of Form

Sunstein, C. (2015) Why nudge? 1st ed. New Haven: Yale University Press.

Thaler, R. and Sunstein, C. (2003) Libertarian Paternalism. American Economic Review, 93(2), pp.175-179.

Tinkler, J. (2011) Designing for nudge effects: how behaviour management can ease public sector problems.

Tversky, A. and Kahneman, D. (1974) Judgment under Uncertainty: Heuristics and Biases. Science, 185(4157), pp.1124-1131.

Thaler, R.H. and Sunstein A (2009) Nudge One Way, A Nudge the Other: libertarian paternalism as Improving decisions about health, wealth and happiness., C.R. London: Penguin.

Thrash, T and Elliot, A (2004) Inspiration: core characteristics, component processes, antecedents and function, J. Pers. Soc. Psychol, vol. 84, p. 957–973.

Wilkinson, T (2013) Nudging and manipulation. Political Studies 61(2): 341–355, https://www.linkedin.com/pulse/20141102132316-72002586-what-is-nudging-and-some-real-world-applications-of-nudging/, Accessed: 12/4/2018.

CHAPTER SIX

Reviewing Implications of 'BE' on Our Future Life[6]

6.1 Introduction

With the development of human psychology, many scientists and especially economists started to believe that presuming that people may depart from rationality could create new measurable theories in the future. However, due to human complexity, we still find debates from the classical economists that more theories are needed to prove the generalisation of the possibility of human irrationality.

If we take for example the study of Heimer et al. (2015) of how young people save too little, and the elderly spend too little, the explanation that old people want to pass money to their children, and that young people do not realise how long they are going to live and spend like there is no tomorrow, if still a puzzle today and if not solved could become more complex in the future.

---

[6] Buheji, M (2019) Reviewing Implications of "Behavioural Economics" on Our Future Life, Issues in Social Science, Vol.7, No.3. pp.9-17.

If BE scientist did this study, they would not try to explain the phenomena, without first setting up first intervention labs to change the seen outcome. This would mean a future where youth knows more about the essentials of savings, whereas the elderly would enjoy their savings and the rest of their time with a high quality of life (Buheji, 2018d).

6.2 Research Framework

This chapter is built on the possible interactions of BE and its type of influence in the future. The fundamental issue here is built on how to optimise BE practices to help address future needs. Therefore, each subject of BE in the literature review is examined from two perspectives:

a- What is the BE position today?
b- Where BE might go in the future?

Both (a) and (b) should help us to understand what are the implications of BE on our socio-economies in the future.

6.3 Literature Review

6.3.1 Pre-BE

Economics is a social science. It is a science that seeks the truths about production, distribution, consumption, wealth accumulation and related tasks through abstraction of observations and analysis.

Neoclassical economics (NE) is built on the assumption that humans are rational, with the proposition that economic behaviour can be described by the mathematical model without the need for inter-disciplinary interference or explanations.

NE and utilitarianism found to be too narrow and does not reflect human needs and behaviour. Therefore, there was more increasing demand for the cognitive state.

6.3.2 Behavioural Macroeconomics

Akerlof (2001) mentioned six phenomena or assumptions that the behavioural macroeconomics would try to change. The first assumption in the New Classical model is that the unemployed worker can quickly obtain a job by offering to work for just a smidgeon less than the market-clearing salary or wage. The other assumption which Akerlof tried to refute the impact of monetary policy on output and employment.

Akerlof saw that if unemployment above the natural rate, inflation continually decelerates. Besides, Akerlof has seen that assuming the prevalence of undersaving for retirement is not totally accurate as today, there are many forced saving programs.

Akerlof seen stock prices does not necessarily reflect the value of future income streams and not necessarily we have a self-destructive underclass and that neoclassical theory cannot account for different causalities of extreme poverty.

Akerlof emphasised the inter-disciplinary approach for Behavioural Macroeconomics using reciprocity, fairness, identity, money illusion, loss aversion, herding and procrastination as techniques that ease transformation from NE (Akerlof, 2001).

Hence, one could synthesis that behavioural macroeconomics (BM) targets to improve how people react to the economic cycle. For example, BM would be concerned about how people prepare, or react to big recessions, and what is its impact on their own lifetimes. BM scientists can help to calibrate the unjustified optimism to optimise the speed of recovery in the future. The outcome expected from BM would be how to build more resilience economy practices that would absorb any repeated economic and socio-economic spikes in the future, so that not to repeat what countries as Greece and Venezuela experienced (Tomer, 2017; Akerlof, 2001).

6.3.3 History of BE

BE started to emerge since the 1950s as a concern of the way NE is developing, i.e. far away from human behavioural explanations and multi-disciplinary interactions. The idea behind BE is to be open up to the new dynamics of life and to adopt new methodologies in economics that help understand the outcome of human decisions.

The history of economics before BE used to be divided into classical and neoclassical. Neoclassical also can be divided into two periods early and post-world war II (Tomer, 2017).

With the development of Nudge, one could see that BE could spread more in communities and would come to be universal phenomena. For example, it became normal today that people or the consumers, or the community being nudged to choose a low-calorie meal, or to save money each month, or to donate their blood or organs. This surely is going to have a positive effect on architecting our decisions. However, all the advanced BE tools are optimised and used more in neuro-marketing, more than any discipline. It is increasing our consumerism diseases (Thaler & Sunstien, 2008).

In a nutshell, the future of BE tools would depend on its simplicity and its low implementation cost, besides its unique outcome in behavioural change (Tomer, 2017).

6.3.4 Influence of BE on Scientific Research and Knowledge Community

Over the years and especially since the 1970's, more economists started to utilise the methods that were developed by the behavioural economists, and blend it with the experimental economic approaches. Buheji (2018c) emphasis that this helped to bring new economies as social, sharing, collaborative, knowledge, innovation, creative, inspiration, resilience and youth economy (Buheji, 2019).

The pragmatic empirical studies published by BE scientists led many scientists from different disciplines to rethink about the same changes required for their own field, especially those been following the same approaches for long years. BE built several related meanings.

BE shown that many assumptions need to be reviewed or dealt with carefully, as presuming that people act from self-interest or that people are always rational in their decisions. Actually, now rigid studies show that Adam Smith himself was highly interested in humans' psychology and what makes them happy, but later economists became busy with theories and formulas (Angner & Loewenstein, 2007).

6.3.5 BE and the Future of Welfare

BE is expected to enhance people, communities and governments economic and socio-economic literacy and thus to help them take charge of their challenging or turbulent environment (Buheji, 2018a).

In the future, BE scientists are expected to take their labs experiments and analysis steps further by measuring the impact of the communities' welfare and not only individuals or government policies. Already recently, we started to find studies that focus on energy conservations, improving charity donation and other positive deeds through managing their psychological cost. BE as per Buheji (2018b) need to focus more on social psychology that would lead to more successful models that would lead to community development and resilience in socio-economic capacity (Buheji, 2018 b, c).

6.3.6 BE and Future Public Policies

If BE continues to develop, it will evolve it would help public policies to target complex and chronic issues, and this would influence both the mindset of the public authorities official and the beneficiary citizens alike. With the development of modern technology such as artificial intelligence Artificial Intelligence (AI) is expected to offer an entirely new possibility of how BE could be delivered across different communities. It would be feasible, for example, to personalise the solutions and options of architecting decisions according to a specific group of citizens or type of individuals (Buheji, 2018c).

6.3.7 BE and Future Consumers Decisions

With the development of neuro-marketing and BE, the retailers could use the information of the consumers and feed it to the algorithms to create specific strategic, sales planning, marketing and distribution decision. If this consumer information used for creating welfare effects.

BE scientists made an analogy to Darwin's model and its differential effects on the routine of behavioural patterns and the life cycle of the selected industry. Nelson and Winter (1985) use inter-disciplinary approaches and organisational that triggers cognitive psychology, and thus, it has more potential to influence our life in our future. One of the implications of such theory is that it helps to the ease the transformation of many industries and their resilience in uncertain times.

The evolutionary theory could also help people to adapt faster to rhythms of technological changes which can enhance the organisation and the communities economic and socio-economic propositions (Buheji, 2018b).

Emotions found to influence economic decision making. Our fear, anger, hunger, thirst and pain all found to be related to how engage in specific economic behaviour. Our consumption is influenced by our emotions (Tomer, 2017).

6.3.8 The Demands for BE Labs in Future

Thanks to BE and neuroscience development; there are today more demands for lab experiments, such as behavioural labs, or inspiration labs than ever before. Now more scientists and researchers realise how effective people economically behave in the real world and where such labs would bring in a type of economic data that can be tested (Buheji, 2019).

In order to foresight BE implications in the future we need to measure, for example, in labs how the behaviour of the consumers or the beneficiaries would deviate from full rationality and how to reduce the effect of their psychological biases.

In summary, lab experiments have become a substantive field of inquiry which led to more spread of the BE in different fields and scopes.

3.9 Bounded Rationality

BE is closely associated with the work of Herbet Simon (1992). Simon seen on that BE is a collection of inter-disciplinary social sciences made mainly from economics, psychology, management, sociology, besides philosophy which all help to understand the human decision making.

Bounded rationality can be the right partner for managing the speed of life in the future, as more rationality in decision-making needs to be intelligent and sensible. This can be achieved through choosing a reasoned, and purposeful manners. This means that future decision-makers would have good alternatives and choices of outcomes.

3.10 Role of Psychological Economy in Future

Psychological Economy (PE), which was proposed by Daniel Kahneman (2011), Nobel Prize Winner, and Amos Tversky in (1982). PE is about the application of cognitive psychology on decision making, i.e. excluding moods and feelings. PE helped and could help more in modelling of economics and cognitive science.

The need for well-defined preferences that maximise the expected utility and create a discount for future wellbeing would still continue to be the primary differentiation for PE. PE help to realise the type of human judgements biases. PE focus on improving the availability of specific instances and how it can be brought to mind. This should improve the BE related to risks, resilience, co-existence, persistence and inspiration (Kahnman et al., 1982).

Anchoring, a type of detection for bias judgement and adjustments, is another contribution of PE towards BE. With anchoring, the BE's can plan to correct the behaviour of valuing or decisions that are made on estimations (Kahnman et al., 1982). This is very important as people who are influenced by arbitrary anchors are increasing due to development of technology and social media. Also, such anchoring can be used for studying the flow of decision making with a particular type of group, i.e. particular age, discipline, etc. PE also focus on representativeness that reflects the probabilistic that a particular type would take a certain decision or go in specific economic direction (Kahnman et al., 1982).

By understanding PE, we could understand more how to deal with two types of thinking: automatic thinking, called system 1, and reflective thinking, called system 2. Kahneman (2011) believes that thinking as System 1 is intuitive and instinctive, i.e. it needs little thinking efforts. While system 2 need deliberate thinking, orderly attention and self-control. This type of thinking would be in more demand in the future due to the complexity in socio-economic life (Buheji, 2018b).

Since Kahneman (2011) shown that most of the time we operate and are presumably influenced by intuitive and automatic mode; with this fast-thinking mode, chances are very high in the future that we would have more heuristics decision that increase would rapidly increase our biases. Hence, in the future PE is expected to be used more in selective deliberate thinking which can create a change that could define how the fast and slow types of thinking could be used in BE designs.

Now more studies are showing minimal attentive effort in dealing with day to day problems could help to improve our decisions more and more in future. Buheji (2018 a, b) emphasised the importance of these attentive efforts through inspiration labs. Buheji saw that inspiration labs help to improve the attentive thinking of the concerned parties by engaging them in socio-economic issues. Such inspiration labs helped to confirm that PE would continue to help people to learn to reduce their biases through being engaged with their environmental challenges and conditions (Buheji, 2019).

PE brought the prospect theory (PT), which focuses on how to deal with gains and losses, such as changes in wealth or welfare from a reference point, Tomer (2017). This lead to what is called 'loss aversion' which measure how people value gains and losses. BE using PT would help to overcome many status quo decisions that stagnate many economic and socio-economic development today and in the future. By overcoming the inertia in the consumer or the beneficiary mindset, the value of the gains could win over the value of the losses. This is highly needed for human development (Buheji, 2018b).

BE also could use more in the future feelings of the endowment effect, where people who possess an object or value can use it more than those who are not endowed. PE helps the consumer to overcome the pain associated with the loss of particular possession to encourage more flow of decisions. The mug study reported by Kahnman (2011) shows that BE could be used in enhancing the consumers' decisions regarding what they possess.

The other PE contribution to BE is framing. With framing, we can direct specific decisions in dealing with socio-economic problems and challenges in a specific way. Through framing with can reduce the rational choices. Studies show that different framing may impose different automatic reactions, i.e. more provoking and stimulation of system 1 thinking. Through such framing BE can take people towards focusing on monetary losses, or towards gain attentions. Hence, the selection of specific statements or facts would direct more people towards specific decisions, based on the framing of the mind towards feeling the losses or the gains. Kahneman and Tversky (2000).

Finally, PE help also to establish mental accounting tools where the BE's could use more in the future for deciding specific customised mental decisions relevant to dealing with problems that require self-control. This could be applied to encourage people saving to specific challenges, as demand for educational expenses, or healthcare services, later retirement.

6.4 Discussion and Concluding Remarks

This chapter examined the future of BE through understanding the economic influence of both rational and irrational decisions. Tomer (2017) has serviced as the main reference book for this review. Tomer book found to be a useful reference for the introduction of BE. However, one has to disagree with the title of the Tomer book as being '"Advanced" Introduction to Behavioural Economy".

Despite the behavioural judgment, biases or errors found to differ in people. Therefore, the future socio-economic influence of BE is foresighted to play a significant effect in architecting our future preferences or solve complex socio-economic problems in relevant to decision or quality of life, women empowerment, children development, youth migration, elderly care, entrepreneurial challenges, etc. This means we can address many problems or re-invent our communities' opportunities with minimal resources, Buheji (2018 a, b, c, d).

The foresight of the future carries lots of potential for BE implementations that can help to map-out our socio-economic development. More studies in the future are expected about how people make decisions.

This chapter shows that there is now a growing body of evidence about the unsuitability of many of the current economic assumptions that call for BE. In order to foresight, the fate of BE in the future more default options that facilitate self-control need to be highlighted and communicated. The findings of this research highlight that many of BE emerging practices would be utilised more by future business actors. The future would depend on the capacity of finding new ways of spreading BE through social interactions.

In the future, we can separate inconsistent choices based on cost-benefit analysis. BE underscores problems relevant to instinctive judgements, thus would suggest ways of improving our decisions.

References

Akerlof, G. (2001). *Behavioural Macroeconomics and Macroeconomic Behavior.* Lecture of Akerlof delivered in Stockholm, Sweden, on Prize in Economic Sciences of Alfred Nobel. The Nobel Foundation. Retrieved from http://socsci2.ucsd.edu/~aronatas/project/academic/akerlof_AER.pdf

Angner, E., & Loewenstein, G. F. (2007). Behavioural Economics. *Handbook of the Philosophy of Science: Philosophy of Economics* (pp. 641-690), Uskali Mäki ed., Amsterdam: Elsevier, 2012. https://doi.org/10.1016/B978-0-444-51676-3.50022-1

Buheji, M. (2019). The Trust Project' Building better accessibility to Healthcare Services through BE and Inspiration Labs. *International Journal of Economics, Commerce and Management, 7*(2), 526-535.

Buheji, M. (2018a). BE Trends in Improving Governments Outcomes – Much More than Nudge. *American Journal of Economics, 8*(3), 163-173.

Buheji, M. (2018b). Nudge Theory vs. Inspiration Economy Labs- Comparing the Depth of Influence on Socio-Economics Behaviours. *American Journal of Economics, 8*(3), 146-154.

Buheji, M. (2018c). *Re-Inventing Our Lives, A Handbook for Socio-Economic "Problem-Solving"*. AuthorHouse, UK.

Buheji, M. (2018d). Understanding the Potential of BE on Establishing 'Quality of Life' Constructs. *American Journal of Economics, 8*(6), 279-288.

Heimer, R. Z., Myrseth, K. O. R., & Schoenle, R. S. (2015). *YOLO: Mortality beliefs and household finance puzzles*. Working Papers 15-21, Federal Reserve Bank of Cleveland. https://doi.org/10.26509/wp-201521

Kahneman, D., Solvic, P., & Tversky, A. (1982). *Judgment Under Uncertainty: Heuristics and Biases*. New York: Cambridge University Press. https://doi.org/10.1017/CBO9780511809477

Kahneman, D., & Tversky, A. (2000). *Choices, Values and Frames*. New York: Cambridge University Press. https://doi.org/10.1017/CBO9780511803475

Kahneman, D. (2011). Thinking, Fast and Slow, Farrar, Straus and Giroux.

Nelson, & Winter. (1985). *An Evolutionary Theory of Economic Change*. Belknap Press: An Imprint of Harvard University Press (October 15).

Thaler, R., & Sunstien, C. (2008). *Nudge: Improving Decisions about Health, Wealth, and Happiness*. Yale University Press.

Tomer, J. (2017). *Advanced Introduction to BE*. E-Elgar.

CHAPTER SEVEN

Practices of Future Foresight in Management of Non-Communicable Diseases : An Early Attempt towards Focusing on 'Foresight Economy' Labs[7]

7.1 Introduction

This chapter shall study the exploration efforts of FELs that targets to establish future practices that would improve the quality of life by the early detection of citizens with Non-Communicable Diseases (NCD's) risk factors, to prevent chronic disease and reduce the mortality from cardiovascular diseases. This early detection shall be called exploration. The target of the exploration

---

[7] Buheji, M (2018) Practices of Future Foresight in Management of Non-Communicable Diseases -An Early Attempt towards Focusing on 'Foresight Economy' Labs. Advances in Social Sciences Research Journal. Vol.5, No.4, pp. 344-355.

is to create a significant development in the country that would complement the current growth effort.

Many rich developed and developing countries are having many distributed healthcare services that take the role of NCD's clinics. However, almost all of these countries suffer the continuous alarming increase of NCD's in the last four decades to the extent it became like an accepted norm in the communities of many parts of the world.

The instability in trends and ratios reflects the lack of regularity of exploring NCD patients during non-NCD clinics. This lacking of capacity to pull patients before reaching the stage where they are totally diseased with one of the NCD's showed an excellent opportunity for mitigation of NCD's risks in future generations. This could be achieved with a foresight lab that shows the socio-economic of NCD's if they continue to spread with the same speed and rate. It is called for short Foresight Economic Lab (FEL).

The FEL focus on optimising the knowledge assets of all the community members in dealing with risk factors of such chronic diseases. The foresight of the future can help in tackling one of the most significant challenges our humanity would face in the next three to five decades that is control of NCD's over the quality of our extended life.

The lab which targets to mitigate NCD's risks was established in Bahrain in coordination with primary health care in the Ministry of Health. Cardiovascular disease, diabetes, respiratory diseases, and cancer all are diseases that is directly and indirectly to NCD's, were considered the top four reason, or killers of Bahraini citizens. The FEL focused on improving the effectiveness of knowledge assets in the areas of exploration, prevention and early detection of risk factors citizens through different techniques. The goal of FEL is to mitigate the potential increase of chronic diseases that would lead to the stretching of treatment services to highly expensive and daunting results.

The FEL focused on developing a culture of early detection in the next twenty years using pull techniques, i.e. early explorations, that could outreach people with potential risks, in collaboration with schools, community centres, health centres, private hospitals, major shopping centres and media. However, the leading player in this long term campaign was and still is the healthcare services staff in CHC's starting from the health visitor, social worker, paramedical staff and family physicians. FEL made the CHC's staff feel the threat and to appreciate the potential positive change they could do for reducing the risks of their community through implementing End-Customer-End technique that was developed during the FELs. 'End-Customer-End' helps the healthcare staff to work as a team that targets to increase their hit rate in discovering potential future NCD's patients through empathetic mindset, i.e. a mindset that feels and addresses the ultimate needs of the customers and not their wants only. This means that discovering or exploring those patients with NCD's risks is more important for their benefit and the sake of future generations. End-Customer-End, therefore, works on satisfying society needs and not only current patient satisfaction with the daily services only.

In order to enhance the capacity for exploration, the services of NCD's where separated between past-current and future patient services. The efforts for chronically ill patients who need the quality of life were separated from the more essential future foresight efforts in relevant to most of the citizens who are likely to have a chronic illness with the development of lifestyle and increase in ages.

Citizens awareness programs shifted from just focusing on practices of learning how to avoid chronic diseases and NCD's, to more focusing on self-exploratory about NCD's risks possibility and directly reporting this to CHC's. This meant an increase in the detection capacity of NCD's symptoms services through the same human assets but with creative exploitation and exploration.

A communication model was established to enhance the catchment of any potential NCD's risk patients floating between private clinics, health centres, government hospital, public schools, chronic diseases clinics and records departments. The clear challenging target for all was to catch 8 out of 10 general patients visiting any of the mentioned clinics, or services and identify which type of risk they carry and then identify a tracking record for them.

The project targeted to minimise people with chronic diseases by 2030 through FEL's early detection based on pull thinking, then identify the risk factors leading to these diseases and try to illuminate them through FEL's again. Codification of patients with NCD's risks was applied in order to minimise patients with potential coming complications from NCD's chronic diseases and to drive away patients from risks leading to number one killer complication, i.e. cardiovascular diseases.

The NCD's exploration FEL targeted to minimise the high demand on the emergency beds, compared to the percentage of the population in the next 20 years and thus minimise the need for hospitalisation. The focus of this FEL were two parts (early detection + NCD risk-free educated, healthy citizens).

7.2 Literature Review

7.2.1 Defining the Importance of Strategic Foresight for Socio-Economic Challenges

Richard Slaughter (2012) defines strategic foresight (SF) is about maintaining a high-quality, coherent and functional forward view to detect adverse conditions, guide policy and shape strategies. While it is impossible to predict the future, SF found to help to analyse the future environment and develop its capability for responding to future challenges.

Harvard's Andrew Leigh (2003) seen that such SF brings in different perspectives that help in broadening governments and public sector menu of policies and services. This is maybe mainly due that SF found to involve options and future scenarios that might affect today's decisions.

Godet (2008) seen that SF plays a role in raising the capacity of any process through moving the community or the organisation mindset from analysis of the environment to studying the possible alternatives for the strategic vision for the future. The foresight makes the mindset questions what scenarios could be applied? What are the strategic options? Moreover, what are the strategic decisions? Such questions help to define what the organisation stands for and what they aim to do.

The practices and purposes of foresight work quite naturally depending on the business or issue in question. Obviously, accurate foresight can help you in building long-term scenarios and in guiding your strategic targets and road-mapping. Foresight is also about tracking foreseeable changes in consumer sentiment and behaviour. Thus, you may identify new opportunities (or risks) even in the short term.

Therefore, the purpose of any strategic foresight when tackling a socio-economic issue could be first turning the changes in the business environment to the own issue advantage. The second purpose of SF, when tackling socio-economic change, is about setting a direction that would focus the efforts on what the future environment will be like and why. Therefore, SF requires continuously new updates about the future and how it would affect the specific working methods across all organisation levels.

SF link the mission, purpose, effectiveness, performance to the bottom line of the business or the issue tackled. As times change, so may the organisation's purpose and therefore, this step is essential to designing strategy which conforms to the aim. To answer the question 'what could happen? It involves the development of possible scenarios for the future. This is done by first scanning the environment in order to discern patterns and trends.

7.2.2 The Holistic Approach of Strategic Foresight

Strategic Foresight is about combining methods of futures work with those of strategic management. It is about understanding upcoming external changes concerning internal capabilities and drivers. Market Foresight is about the consideration of possible and probable futures in the organisation's relevant business environment, and about identifying new opportunities in that space. This is simply because thinking across current industry boundaries is today an essential source of innovation.

Strategic Foresight is a concept about mirroring the possible and potential futures against the understanding of organization-specific capabilities, and those of one's competitors. Ultimately, Strategic Foresight is about the strategic choices you make based on this combination of external and internal insight.

There lots of recent work that tries to study the basis of the strategic foresight, one of which is the work of Hines and Gold (2013). SF can be categorised to be based on the historical events, evolving paradigms and new waves of predictive perspectives. SF also can become from interpretive studies, critical action learning as per studies of Slaughter (2012).

7.2.3 The Challenges of Strategic Foresight

A strategic decision is either one that creates an irreversible situation, or it would anticipate an environmental change that would provoke an irreversible situation. In light of this definition, the setting an SF means departing from the status quo and this is usually challenging. The limitations for considering SF, is ambiguity, reluctance to change, unwillingness to objectively view reality and risk, which would help to frame the concept and its usefulness before attempting to apply it. Hines et al. (2017) describe SF as differentiation from typical business challenge through trying to eliminate the ambiguity which is likely to cause doubt about the usefulness of the process.

Other coming psychological challenges on how might we best manage our memories and mobilise the past to enhance the wellbeing of the community in the future. Situational awareness and consideration of the future, even if it does not yield a single concrete way-ahead, will enable the concerned parties to be more aware of environmental changes and be prepared to react to indications more rapidly.

7.2.4 Improving the NCD's Exploration Process

All the healthcare staff mentioned (from health visitors till family physicians) were ready for the early detection of patients both through physical analysis and then in-depth screening. A standard form for cases of early detection was conducted. Specifically, the family physicians were asked to choose 10 people from their daily list of up to 50 patients to meet a hit rate of 90%.

If a person is diagnosed with a non-chronic disease and is irregular in treatment, he / she is referred to a non-communicable disease clinic. While people detected with NCD's risk are referred to the health educator to work with them as a mentor.

7.2.5 FEL is about Projection of better Hit Rate

In order to decrease the severity of NCD's risks and decrease their probability of occurrence or control, as per the formula: *Risk=probability x severity*, FEL was designed to enhance the practice of hit rate.

Despite all the world-class appreciated primary care services and variety of care clinics, including NCD's specific clinics, as diabetes clinic, obesity clinic, blood pressure management

'Behavioural Economics'

clinic and nutrition clinic to decrease the risks to NCD's, the capacity for early detection of risk factors was fragile. Besides, the lack of adherence to clinical guidelines for early detection, the primary care staff had low monitoring of detected cases and poor follow-up to the persons exposed to the risk of NCD's.

Through FEL, a standardized system for early detection of risk factors was developed where registration form is designed to ensure monitoring of detected cases in order to convert the path flow of people at risk of any of the NCD's. Patients explored with early detection of risks of NCD's complications were thoroughly explained the other complication that comes with it, as heart stroke, body stroke, blindness, total renal failure and even amputations.

FEL helped to develop a type of competition for early detection methods and confining the proportion of NCD's patients who might go to the risk of heart diseases without being detected. FEL found that the proportion of diabetic patients are beyond those 35.7% with controlled diabetes and hypertensive patients are beyond the 47.8% with controlled pressure. FEL helped in discovering the risk factors of the community and reducing the beneficiaries of all types of clinics in relevance to non-communicable diseases who are in need of health centre 8.9%.

Percentage of newly discovered patients with NCD's per doctor per day increased from below 1% to 25% in just the first few days. This exploration effort was working in parallel to the efforts of improving NCD's clinics' appointment system from an average of a month to less than two hours. The home visits awareness program increased for selective families with NCD's patients. The screening throughput process of probable NCD risk patients also reduced from 2.5 hours to 20-30 minutes.

The number of patients whose risk factors were detected / total number of patients attending public clinics reached 40%. While the number of diabetes patients with controlled diabetes/ total Diabetics patients reached 43%. In the other hand, the number of hypertensive patients with controlled pressure/ total patients with hypertension reached 48%.

Duration of the actual consultation for patients with NCD risks was increased after six months from starting the program in the model CHC. Time allotted for risk identified NCD's now is more comfortable.

The FEL built a system of communication and the periodic review and knowledge-sharing groups for the reduction of the chronic disease in all Bahrain. The long objective FEL is to promote the lifestyles necessary for patients in the region and periodically. An agreement was also made with the emergency team to follow NCD's cases once identified with risks.

7.2.6 FEL Outcomes

Risk factors for NCD's found to be correlated with physical inactivity, unhealthy food, bad practices as smoking and drinking alcohol, obesity and high cholesterol. The early detection through effective exploration would help to manage these bad practices earlier and thus mitigate the risk of the coming generation, away from chronic diseases. The idea is to raise the (capacity vs demand) through early exploration of risk factors that lead to these NCD's. This would help to develop a future, within 20 years, of citizens with minimal complications from chronic diseases and thus reducing also the cardiovascular-related diseases that mostly leads to emergency beds and thus the need for hospitalisation.

The FEL enhanced peers training in the management of chronic patient through effective management of actual consultation time. Chronic diseases clinic now takes on average only approximately 12 minutes with nurses and 6 minutes with the physician and wait 5 minutes for it to continue.

7.2.7 Sustaining FEL Outcomes

While strategic foresight processes have been largely examined in the context of private sector companies, little has been written about the future of the public sector, Dove (2012). Through the strategic foresight, we can re-examine the public organisation's aim and objectives in light of the possible future scenarios in order to make informed decisions about the direction of the organisation.

The establishment of the Risk Factors Clinic (RFC) came to support the efforts and the raising of the capacity for early exploration. This reduced the patients' overall journey for diagnosis to be 10 minutes and a designation of a followup plan with the nurses to only 8 minutes.

Before the kick-off of the FEL, the high cost of treatment of NCD's was expected to multiply at least three times by 2050, despite the advancement of the technology. The continuous high population growth rate and extension of the life expectancy at birth would continue to create a substantial-high demand on the primary health services and thus it would have influenced its capability in creating compelling exploration for those prone to NCD's risks in next 30 years.

Dealing with the future in construction of more advanced health centres and hospitals would not have solved the rising percentages of NCD's among the population. The catchment of 9 out of 10 patients targeted by each family physician in the first CHC and then the next 5 CHC's whom spread the model of early detection through focused exploration, showed that the non-intervention of the future of (20 to 30 years) would have carried even more alarming high incidence of non-communicable diseases and controllable deaths from cardiovascular-related diseases.

Studies of GCC and specifically Bahrain history showed that in the last three decades and despite again the high advancement of primary care clinics and related early detection services, patients of high blood pressure increased by 12%, the diabetic disease increased 14.3% while the cholesterol level patients increased by 40.6%. In the same time weight gain and obesity amongst the citizens increased by 36.3%, where lack of physical activity increased by 57.1%. Besides the tobacco consumption increased by 19.9% amongst young generations. Other complications of NCD's have been on the rise. For example, diabetes leads to an increase of heart and brain attacks, kidney failure, blindness, neuropathy, difficulty in healing wounds and amputation of the limbs.

7.2.8 Process of Establishing a Specific Context Foresight

Foresight is more than ideational; it is regarded as a communication tool and a key towards achieving higher organisational, or community impact or even outcome. Foresight according to Gergen (1985) is a social construction, a methodology by which we can make an account for the world in which we live in. Therefore, the exercise of foresight establishes a process of interaction and meanings that can be embedded into the accepted versions of reality. With foresight, the collected macro trends of the context under focus help to provide orientation for the decision-makers and stakeholders (Rollwagen, et al. 2008). Therefore, foresight is thought to focus on the future, while dealing with it as a reality of today. Be it anticipation of social, health, economic, political and/or technological trends; the foresight exercise will help to shape the strategic decisions needed to deliver better results to the concerned parties.

Daheim and Urez (2008) specified that foresight starts with future intelligence-gathering how the process can be widespread in a specific business context and through different methodologies. Foresight, as seen by Henshel (1981), looks for stages of social construction in a holistic way, but in a specific context. Foresight can help in overcoming different challenges to overcome a specific impact that was affecting the current business decision-making (Rollwagen et al., 2008).

There have been many studies about the best-structured way of producing and delivering a specific context foresight in relevance to a proper time perspective (Rollwagen, et al., 2008). Foresight can be drawn from the organisational procedures, goals and practice. Alternatively, it can come from the result of the different levels of interaction with decision-makers.

7.2.9 Understanding the future challenge of Non-Communicable Diseases

WHO defined that most of the deaths in the future would continue to come from the Non-Communicable Diseases (NCD's) and even in developed countries as OECD countries. Therefore, Wepner and Giesecke (2018) seen that NCD's such as cardiovascular problems, diabetes, cancer, multi-skeletal disorders, depression and neurologic disorders would be the leading causes of deaths, but would develop earlier as diseases among underprivileged people in Europe in the last thirty years.

In a vast EU funded foresight project called Foresight and Modelling for European Health Policy and Regulation, called for short (FRESHER), Wepner and Giesecke (2018) showed the influence of NCD's related diseases on the scenarios of policies direction with stakeholders from health, research, care, patient organisations, insurances and policy-making that go beyond the usual activities and pose alternatives that promise to be more successful.

From an analysis of trends that affect NCD's, a future foresight study is needed in the area with a focus on rich developing countries and emerging economies. Today, the focus of the future foresight of these countries became more diverted on national medical insurance programs than on setting plans for more advanced facilities that would absorb the increasing amount of patients.

The unique about the FRESHER study is that it identified socio-demographic development far beyond the usual determinants of tobacco and alcohol consumption, salt, sugar and fat intake, or sedentary behaviours by focusing on scenarios with one comprehensive approach that is "health in all EU policies", Wepner and Giesecke (2018). The significant NCD's trends expected in the next decades helped to The study showed the socio-economic impacts of NCDs that are beyond medical and healthcare services only. Thus Wepner and Giesecke (2018) study show us that management and mitigation of NCD's risk should go beyond the traditional approach of health policy and out of the box thinking is needed to pay tribute to the complexity of future health systems.

The FRESHER study showed that NCD's could influence socio-economic aspects like equity, literacy, mobility or urban planning. Therefore, a systematic and holistic approach is needed in order to address all NCD's drivers and determinants, if countries and communities are expected to enjoy a healthy life and well-being.

7.3 Case Study

7.3.1 Purpose of Case Study.

This case focuses on showing the power of future foresight and *visualisation in shifting a country focus towards quality of life practices* and how to make it less dependent on primary care services only. Through FEL techniques, we show how, with visualisation, *observation data collected* for the early detection of non-communicable diseases (NCDs) visualised outcomes of NCD's influence help to focus the efforts on *enhancement of the*

'Behavioural Economics'

capacity of NCDs' detection. This program influenced many interrelated programs like the family physician program and the triage system in the CHC's. Also, the program helped to enhance the early *detection of* anxiety patients and prioritising emergency care beds.

This project targeted to help the government decision-makers to shift their attention to how to create a country to be one of the top 10 countries health-wise (no lack of exercise, no smoking, good family history, no obesity, etc.), more than just a country with best healthcare facilities and services.

7.3.2 Foresight Methodology

Representation of alternative futures of population with NCD's were simulated with possible emerging health scenarios. The foresight was used to test the future with practices as-is, or when early exploration is done for detecting population with risks of NCD's. Rather than just extrapolating past NCD's trends, the project used FEL 'hit rate' challenge to show the importance of managing the foresighted future of population growth with more risks of NCD's.

The risk for NCDs was illustrated with experts challenging the CHC's staff in workshops as well as in an online survey and subsequently combined in the next step to four scenarios depicting possible futures. The main challenge in the FEL's to define the foresighted determinants that would lead or stay to lead to specific trends with negative health effects that would lead to raising the risks of NCD's and how could they be changed?

Overall, socio-demographic and economic trends were considered to be essential drivers in the reduction of the incidence of NCD's. Citizen empowerment was seen latent factor by first helping them to understand their levels of NCD's risks as early as possible.

7.3.3 Piloting the Early Detection Capacity

A specific health centre was defined for carrying a pilot study of a random sample with 1000 patients to diagnosed on WHO NCD Risk Factor scale of 10 (100%). The patients were from both genders and different occupations. More than 91% were shown to be likely to suffer one of the NCD's in the next ten years. Then, two CHC's were identified to be the model centres that would identify a target population of 50 patients that would have the risk of NCD's in coming future or already being diseased with it without being identified.

7.3.4 Mitigation of NCD's Risks through FEL's

Foresight economy lab (FEL), as shown in Figure (1) illustrates first the socio-economic risks of the increase of the alarming NCD's epidemic risks among all the nation citizens, where more results-based strategic plans put by the healthcare authority and their stakeholders will not lead to real solutions. i.e. Even development of facilities and services in relevance to NCD's clinics and patients might lead to going round the problem and actually solving this epidemic that would deteriorate the quality of many citizens and especially those above 60 years old.

Therefore, with the introduction of FEL a mindset for seeing the foresight economic opportunity would be introduced. An early exploration of potential NCD's risk patients would lead to more outcome-driven future practices. i.e. The capacity would be developed to explore and detect potentials NCD's patients and mitigate their quality of life risks, as shown in Figure (1).

Figure (1) Role of FEL Opportunity in mitigating the NCD's Risks

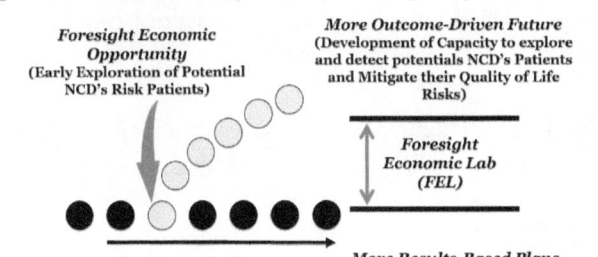

Besides competing in raising the capacity for hit rate, i.e. the percentage of patients identified with risks of NCD's as per WHO scale from the first time, each centre approached a differentiated post-NCD identification protocol. One of the two early models CHC's focused its efforts on working with families, while the other centre focused on the wellness, especially with those patients with a risk factor of fewer than ten years.

Both CHC has worked on the same methodology of changing the lifestyle of the patients and their families. A bundle of programs that focused on improving sleeping, eating, socialising, cutting out or reducing smoking, and, most of all, lightly exercising was mentored through the nurses, the health visitors and social workers. The results were amazing. Both centres managed to reduce those patients with NCD's risk factor of 10 years from being, on average, 80% to 56% (either by pushing them totally out of risk factor 6% or delaying their risk factors to occur in 20 years). The programs helped to reduce the risk factor in 20 years to be pushed towards after 60, especially in 30% of the young patients. In young people, they managed to reduce the risk factors for NCDs in 45% of them and now almost 70% of the young patients identified have their risk factors in the range after 15 till 40 years.

The goal of the project was set to raise the healthcare staff, and the country capacity for the early detection and exploration of NCD's against the % of NCD's citizen discovered late with higher risks symptoms. The time for foresighted future was set to be by 2050, as shown in Figure (2).

Figure (2) The Foresighted Future Challenges of Early Exploration of the NCD's before further Risks Development.

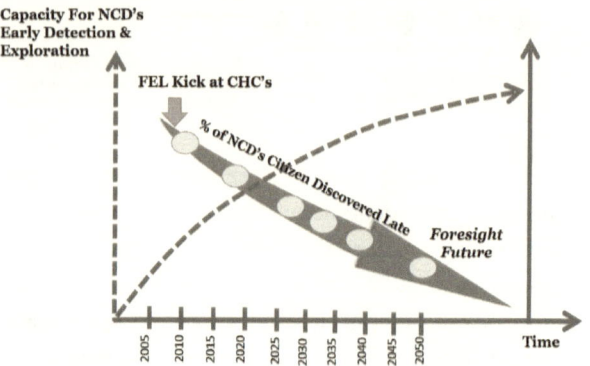

7.3.5 Using the Power of Observation in tackling NCD's

All the participating healthcare staff in CHC's from family physicians to social workers and health visitors were asked to use the power of observation, which is 50% dependent on physical observations without the need for the in-depth analysis, in order to segregate or code and thus screen patients with risks of NCD's. The programme showed that even if considering families with no history of NCDs, we would almost get the same figure (89%) at risk.

The same study was extended to all health centres and later even to the 'Schools Health Programme' where more than 30,000 students from 13 to 18 years old were included. The number again showed a relatively high level compared to the students' ages: i.e., on average, 40% would get NCDs in next 20 years.

There are now more than 32 health centres in which follow this early catchment and exploration programme. The risk factors

'Behavioural Economics'

in the general population and especially amongst those below 20 years old have now dropped from 91% to 82% in just three years, without adding any extra resources.

7.3.6 NCD's Exploration Opportunities

All CHC's staff (i.e. family physicians, nurses, administration staff, health visitors, awareness specialists and social workers) were explained a foresight economy technique that the researcher developed called exploration of opportunities. In order to create their commitment, every member of the team was asked to choose a minimum of 10 patients with a challenge to explore whether they would be prone for any of the NCD's risk in their life. The challenge was that they should get a hit rate of 80% before the in-depth diagnostics. This also meant the family physicians would need to give more authority to nurses, social workers and health visitors to spot NCDs earlier and in order to measure their hit rate.

7.3.7 Improving NCD's Knowledge Management Programme

In order to capture more NCD's risk patients, Knowledge Management (Called NCD's-KM) was implemented. NCD's-KM started with increasing the availability of the health visitor in all highly populated areas, such as shopping centres, etc. around the year. The performance of each of the primary care teams was measured in terms of how they innovate in creating awareness in their potential population. This meant creating knowledge sharing practising communities of collaborative partnership programmes with the involvement of large organisations such as universities, government organisations, etc. and measure their hit rates.

The program helped to develop the knowledge base the percentages of NCD's at risk of those aged between 15 and 75 years. The CHC's team worked together not only to explore, but also to track and analyse in greater depth the type of results of this exploration, such as continuous blood analyses, to help create better forecasting and then make intelligence level decisions in the areas of BMI, high blood pressure, high fasting sugar levels, HBA1C, total cholesterol levels, LDL, HDL and triglyceride levels. The CHC's team started then to share the best practices of patients' NCDs' discovery and management programmes.

7.4 Discussion and Conclusion

This research helped all involved primary healthcare staff working in CHC's from the family physicians, nurses, health visitors, social workers and dieticians; all appreciate the foresighted future if the current practices do not change. The FEL has been used to raise the capacity of those healthcare staff to capture risks of NCD's on the population, especially that in diseases as diabetes, blood pressure, cholesterol and obesity which are spread in the Gulf Cooperation Council (GCC) in general and specifically in Bahrain. The trends and drivers shape transformative scenarios and their potential for future policy options, specifically, how to extend health policy and make it adaptable to current challenges posed by NCD's.

FEL proved to be a sound methodology for improving outcomes in relevance to socio-economic projects as the NCD's exploration project and even in enhancing the Hit Rate for the acceleration of the related outcomes.

Sustaining FEL outcomes through establishing a specific context foresight would help to understand the future challenges of Non-Communicable Diseases (NCD's). FEL might be further explored as a foresight methodology that mitigates a socio-economic problem as NCD's risks on the population through an effective knowledge management programme.

This chapter opens a line for future research on the priority of raising the capacity of the healthcare staff by making them foresight the results of their deeds and contemporary practices. The research gives lots of lessons of the role of FEL in improving the learning by doing projects and how it helps to create a management of change for the mindset of healthcare professionals and in the same time improves the future extended health policies.

The limitation of the research is that it did not show the risks of NCD's on the future society performance, and how the improvement of the health policies of early exploration of NCD's amongst the population would help in the meeting the Sustainable Development Goals on NCDs.

References

Boisot, M and McKelvey, B (2006) Speeding Up Strategic Foresight in a Dangerous and Complex World: A Complexity Approach. Chapter 3 in *Corporate Strategies Under International Terrorism and Adversity*. Cheltenham & Northampton: Edward Elger.

Daheim, C and Urez, G (2008) Corporate foresight in Europe: from trend-based logics to open foresight, Journal of Technology Analysis & Strategic Management , Vol 20 (3), pp. 321-336

Dove, R (2012) Strategic Foresight in Canadian Forces Development of Armour Capabilities: Pursuing the Horizon? CANADIAN FORCES COLLEGE CSP 38 - PCEMI 38 https://www.cfc.forces.gc.ca/259/290/298/286/dove.pdf, Accessed 7/3/2018.

Godet, M (2008) Strategic Foresight La Prospective: Use and Misuse of Scenario Building. LIPSOR Working Paper, no. 10; http://innovbfa.viabloga.com/files/LIPSOR___Strategic_Foresight.pdf; Accessed 7/3/2018.

Hines, A (2006) The Strategic Foresight; The State of the Art. Futurist 40, no. 5 (September/October): 18-21.

Hines, A and Gold, J (2013) Professionalizing foresight: Why do it, where it stands, and what needs to be done, Journal of Futures Studies, June, 17(4): 35-54. http://jfsdigital.org/wp-content/uploads/2013/10/174-A03.pdf, Accessed:1/2/2018.

Hines, A; Gary, J; Daheim, and Van der Laan, L (2017) Building Foresight Capacity: Toward a Foresight Competency Model World Futures Review, pp. 1–19 July 10, http://www.andyhinesight.com/wp-content/uploads/2017/05/Building-Foresight-Capacity-FINAL-DRAFT.pdf; Accessed 28/1/2018.

Leigh, A (2003) Thinking Ahead: Strategic Foresight and Government. Australian Journal of Public Administration, 62, no. 2; http://people.anu.edu.au/andrew.leigh/pdf/Thinking%20Ahead%20-%20Strategic%20foresight.pdf; Accessed 2/1/2018.

Rollwagen, I; Hofmann, J and Schneider, S (2008) Improving the business impact of foresight, Journal of Technology Analysis & Strategic Management , Vol 20 (3), pp. 337-349

Slaughter, R (2012) Developing and Applying Strategic Foresight. http://www.forschungsnetzwerk.at/downloadpub/2002slaughter_Strategic_Foresight.pdf; Accessed 28/1/2018.

Wepner, B and Giesecke, S (2018) Drivers, trends and scenarios for the future of health in Europe. Impressions from the FRESHER project, European Journal of Futures Research, Dec, 6: 2. https://doi.org/10.1007/s40309-017-0118-4

Weber M, Schaper-Rinkel P, Giesecke S (2017) Futures of research and innovation: transformative scenarios and the dilemma of research and innovation policy. In: Weber M (ed) Innovation, Complexity and Policy. Contributions from 30 years of innovation policy research in Austria. PL Academic Research, Frankfurt/Main, pp 67–81.

CHAPTER EIGHT

Gamification Techniques to Re-Invent Public Healthcare Services – A Case Study[8]

8.1 Introduction

Gamification is an innovative approach that foster motivation in non-game contexts. This chapter investigates how gamification can help in creating change and re-inventing the public healthcare services in any country, taking the context of the healthcare system in the Kingdom of Bahrain. Buheji (2019a), McGonigal (2011).

A review of the different game designs indicators is done after reviewing the concept of gamification and its critical success factors. After that, different motivational perspectives are analysed. Then psychology of gamification design is discussed. Requirements of Gamification in any public services

---

[8] Buheji, M (2019) Gamification Techniques to Re-Invent Public Healthcare Services – A Case Study, International Journal of Human Resource Studies, Vol. 9, No. 2, 339-351.

business model is discussed with a focus on healthcare services. Heckhausen and Heckhausen (2008).

To implement the gamification, the game elements in the re-invented healthcare services are stratified. The theoretical review results are compared to the effectiveness of the re-invented healthcare services design. The motivational and emotional involvement during the healthcare service delivery creates a differentiated influence that is investigated later. The basic idea of gamification in changing healthcare services is to use its motivational power and environment influencing behaviour to foster better learning and awareness. Early research showed that this influence psychological perspective, Buheji (2019a), Deci and Ryan (1985).

8.2 Literature Review

8.2.1 What is gamification, and what differentiate it?

Gamification helps to turn a routine into something exciting through developing better interaction. By turning events into games, we can change many regular tasks into something exciting, and make it easier to learn or sustain a behaviour too. This can be very beneficial for social change. Rughiniş (2013), McGonigal (2011), Deterding et al. (2011).

Gamification is a method that applies the principles of games, and games design techniques into real-life activities. The concept uses the fun and addictive part of games to increase the engagement and motivation of people to achieve specific tasks through optimising status and achievements. Robinson and Bellotti (2013), Heckhausen and Heckhausen (2008).

The sense of games creates urgent optimism with an immediate desire to overcome a challenge while building better relationships. Games create the urge to explore and activates our curiosity to find meaning. Gamification use games design elements which are made of four constructs, which has to be achieved to reach a specific goal while giving feedback about progress towards that goal. Hense and Mandl (2012), McGonigal (2011).

8.2.2 How to Use Gamification for Social Change?

Since the application of gamification is comprehensive, this study focuses on the non-digital realisations in public services, focusing on typical indicators and constructs used in gamification. For example, the constructs create codification, i.e. like colour coding that points to the accumulated activities within the gamification environment. The codification is similar to badges in games which are visual representations of achievements, which can be collected within the gamification environment. Rughiniş (2013), McGonigal (2011).

Visual management is used to resemble the leaderboards in games where the players are listed and usually are ranked by their success. Codification of status of achievement also represents the progress bars are used to provide information about the current status of a player towards a goal. The 'hit rate' is used to resemble performance graphs and to provide information about a players' performance, compared to previous performance. McGonigal (2011).

The gamification also uses 'quests of little tasks' where the stakeholders or the players need to fulfil to sustain a specific task. The gamification design needs to reflect meaningful stories. Robinson and Bellotti (2013), Deterding et al. (2011).

The idea of gamification helps to build self-determination, which creates psychological needs for competence, autonomy, and social relatedness. The fulfilment of these needs fosters intrinsic inspiration which helps people to execute challenging yet exciting service development nature. This helps to effectively and interactively to execute the task that integrates with the targeted needs. Gamification helps to define a way of penalising those who choose to do something poorly. Buheji and Ahmed (2018), Buheji and Ahmed (2017), Ryan and Deci (2000), Skinner (1963).

8.2.3 The Psychology of Gamification Design

If you ask gamification designers about their goals, they will probably tell you is to make the user's life simple. When gamification designers work on a product, they put maximum effort into creating something that gives users the straightest path to their desired outcome.

Organisations are increasingly using gamification in a wide range of applications, but little work has been done to link gamification to psychological trait perspectives that change the behaviours of the targeted group. The gamification addresses the need for power and the need for affiliation. Thus internal processes, such as expectancies, estimations, and assessments, play a significant role in cognitive theories of motivation. McGonigal (2011), Deci and Ryan (1985).

Another psychological variable is performance orientation, and mastery orientation can be differentiated through both exceeding specific standards of peers and then self-defined standards. Skinner (1963).

The mechanisms of motivations make the stakeholders more likely to be motivated to achieve the goals of a given situation and foster mastery orientation regarding these goals. The stakeholders keep getting motivated to discover through experiential learning and thus to build the feeling of competence and autonomy. Sailer et al. (2017), Heckhausen and Heckhausen (2008).

Researchers constitute interest as a motivational variable that is content-specific and evolves in interaction with the environment. At this moment, interest is both an effective and cognitive variable.

Motivational Mechanisms address interest and flow of the stakeholders for the situational context. The stakeholders are likely to be motivated if gamification enhances the feeling of flow by providing direct feedback. Sailer et al. (2017), Heckhausen and Heckhausen (2008).

The perspective of emotion focuses on the roles of emotions in cognitive and motivational processes. Emotions interact with these cognitive and motivational processes and can be influenced by instructional strategies. The stakeholders are likely to be motivated if gamification decreases negative feelings like fear, envy, and anger. In the same, while gamification increases positive feelings like sympathy and pleasure. Werbach and Hunter (2012).

8.2.4 Gamification and Inspiration Labs

Gamification is based on iteration and emotion. Before we gamify any business we need first to understand it, observe the opportunities built in it, reflect our point of view, ideate about, prototype about and do playtesting, Domínguez et al. (2013). This precisely what inspiration labs do when trying to re-invent any business model. Inspiration labs help us to analyse the requirements, do research analysis, establish gamification frameworks, establish interdisciplinary teams, build rapid prototyping and experience playtesting. Buheji and Ahmed (2017), Robinson and Bellotti (2013), Werbach and Hunter (2012).

Buheji (2018) showed how inspiration labs techniques could solve any sophisticated socio-economic problems through the method of observation. Observation target to either find opportunities inside the problem or simplify the transformation by raising the capacity to realise the change in the specific community targeted. Throughout the inspiration lab, active participation, field visits, gamification, networking, surveys, individual and collective reflections are used to enhance the efficacy of observation, as Figure (1) shows.

Figure (1) Illustrates the Gamification as part of the Method of Observation in Inspiration Labs.

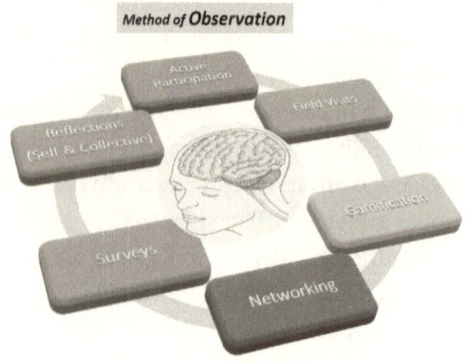

There have been different attempts to create lists of those game elements, which can be applied in gamification. Werbach and Hunter (2012) distinguished between the dynamics of gamification, which constitute the prominent picture aspects, mechanics, which describe the underlying processes, and components, which are specific instantiations of dynamics and mechanics.

Kapp (2012) lists typical game elements like goals, rules conflict, competition, cooperation, time, reward structures, feedback, levels, storytelling, the curve of interest and aesthetics. All these attempts should help to grasp how diverse game elements could look like, but they should be understood as non-exhaustive lists. McGonigal (2011).

8.2.5 Constructs and Indicators of Gamification Techniques

There are main constructs for any gamification design. These key factors are mainly working to ensure the following leading indicators achieved: mechanical indicators, reward indicators, behaviour indicators and measurement indicators. Sailer et al. (2017), Deci and Ryan (1985).

'Behavioural Economics'

The constructs and indicators of gamification are influenced by behavioural game mechanics called in study 'gamification techniques'. The gamification techniques are solely focused on human behaviour and can be in the form: feedback loops, progression, engagement loops, engagement and re-engagement optimisation. Thus these gamification techniques can be like: achievements badges, levels, leaderboards, progress bars, activity feeds, avatars (i.e. ideas for example), real-time feedback, challenges and quests, trophy case and mini-games within other activities. The gamification techniques help to build the gamification construct indicators, be it: mechanical-, rewards-, measurement- and behaviour-based. Hense and Mandl (2012).

1. Mechanical Construct

The first construct focus on mechanical indicators such as visual storytelling, visual cues, response objects, reward schedules, disincentives, access and social feedback.

2. Rewards Construct

The second construct focus on rewards indicators which includes: recognition, status, access and stuff.

3. Measurement Construct

The third construct focuses on rewards indicators which include: reputation, performance, quality, completion, quantity and time.

4. Behaviour Construct

The fourth construct focuses on rewards indicators which include: loyalty, mastery, quality and engagement.

8.2.6 Using Gamification in Public Healthcare Services

In socio-economic problem-solving, we need to introduce gamification without being getting too involved with current restrictions. To encourage interactive healthcare change using gamification for better health and reduced diseases through sustained behaviour change. Buheji (2019a), McGonigal (2011).

Gamification is a great technique that can become an innovative part of our outreach tool kit for a social or behavioural change. Using games and gamification techniques can offer non-profits and public agencies a unique and engaging way to interact with their community to promote change that benefits the individual and society. Rughiniş (2013).

Gamification is becoming more of a scientific approach to social development and change, while it started to influence many decision-makers and have its practical use in socio-economic issues. Gamification is about applying game-based thinking to organisation business, processes or new concepts or brands. Through gamification, we create a new experience about the inherent powers within, including the level of focus, observation and persistence. Ryan and Deci (2000).

Gamification is one of the most essential tools today in changing the mindset of the stakeholders and setting effective strategies for social transformation. Through gamification, we can recognise the level of learning and achievement, with relatively informal and immediate feedback in relevance to day-to-day practice. Gamification found to be particularly crucial in non-formal settings.

Gamification as per Buhijji (2017) is very attractive to human mindset, since it is based on incremental, achievable yet challenging goals, that are tracked by points and personal progress analysis.

8.3 Methodology

A synthesis of the literature for the constructs and indicators of gamification of the public healthcare services was carried out.

Then a list of the inspiration labs projects carried out published by the author in Buheji (2019a) and Buheji (2018) for healthcare services are listed in the table. Then, the type of gamification techniques and constructs used in the inspiration labs projects are categorised according to the type of healthcare services or sectors: primary care, secondary care (hospitals), public health services, health enrichment and psychiatric services. Then, a review of the type gamification constructs that dominates more the re-invented healthcare activities is presented and discussed. The findings focus on the suitability of gamifying such public services activities through such gamification techniques and constructs. Then a discussion and conclusion are drawn based on this finding.

8.4 Case Study

ii. Background about Gamifying the Healthcare Services

During 2010 till 2016, there were more than 17 projects started in the healthcare services in the Kingdom of Bahrain through what is called inspiration labs. The labs targeted to improve and radically change in collaboration with the public healthcare service providers in their main sectors: primary care, secondary care, public health services, community health enrichment services and public health directorates. Buheji (2018).

Buheji (2018) mentioned all these public healthcare services labs where different gamification approaches were used in relevance to the type of exploration or opportunities utilised. For example, one of the labs focused on the early detection of Non-Communicable Diseases (NCD's), i.e. WHO listed central cardio-vascular related disease: diabetes, blood pressure, cholesterol and obesity. The labs targeted raising the capacity of all the healthcare staff and integrating their efforts in discovering the NCD's patients as early as possible. This led to using gamification techniques that would help to expand the responsibility of healthcare staff through a competition technique called 'Hit Rate". The idea of the 'Hit-Rate' was to gamify the sense of visual measurement and reward at the end of each day, Domínguez et al. (2013). Each healthcare staff: family physicians, nurses, assistant nurses, healthcare visitors and social workers were asked to compete on quantity and quality of catchment of the NCDs patients, as part of their day to day processes and services. Measurement whiteboards were set in each clinic and treatment rooms to ensure the percentage of NCDs discovered, i.e. percentage of hit rate, compared to the number of patients diagnosed or treated or serviced. The results affected the spread of the project throughout all the health centres as it became evident that with the available resources, the percentages of NCDs risk discovery can increase considerably. This project helped to manage the risk of NCD can start early and can help mitigate the risk of the disease to a later stage in life or avoid it.

iii. 5.2 Type of Gamification Techniques

Similar to what reviewed and presented in section 3.5, there are more techniques also that are suitable to gamifying the services, as in the healthcare case. For example, this case used techniques as the 'Hit Rate' and codification besides the techniques listed in 3.5. Therefore, the different types of gamification techniques used in the 21 types of labs conducted during four years, in the five healthcare sectors are represented in the third column in Table (1). The table shows how the type of gamification techniques addresses one of the gamification constructs indicators for each type of lab. For example, we would see that labs used, for example, Hit Rates, others used Stickers or batches, etc. Deterding et al. (2013)

Table (1) links all the different healthcare services or sectors to the gamification techniques and constructs indicators.

'Behavioural Economics'

Table (1) Gamification Techniques used in Healthcare Services Activities

Type of Healthcare Services	Type of Gamification Activities Used in the Inspiration Labs Projects/ Models	Gamification Techniques	Constructs Indicators
26. Primary Care	1-Early detection of Non-Communicable Diseases (NCD's), i.e. Diabetes, Blood Pressure, Cholesterol and Obesity through expanding responsibility of healthcare staff and defining of 'Hit-Rate' Competition. 2-Enhancement of Quality through Inspiring Families Physicians. 3-Codifying Patients Self-Triage according to their level of emergency and priority of the case in health-centres. 4-Codify physicians in their capacity for early detection of Psycho-Sematic in relevance to Anxiety in Health Centre. 5-Increase the Health centres readiness for Emergency Cases.	Hit-Rate Codification Speed Batches Calibration Codification Alertness Error-Proofing Leader-boards Levels Interactions Response Alertness Interactions	Visual Storytelling (1) Access and stuff (2) Status (2) Performance (3) Response objects (1) Quality and engagement (4)

Type of Healthcare Services	Type of Gamification Activities Used in the Inspiration Labs Projects/ Models	Gamification Techniques	Constructs Indicators
	6-Optimising the role of Social Workers and Health Educational Specialist and Health visitors in family screening.	Progress bars	Reward scheduling (1)

Quantity and time (3) |
	7-Classifying the type of patients' time spent with physicians as per NCDs Risk Matrix.	Establishing avatars	Reputation (3)
	9-Stream-mapping healthy practices in Educational Institutions towards 'NCD free Generations'.	Activity Feeds	
	10-Gauging the Development of the capacity to analyse the Family Profile Competition between Health Centres.		
27. Secondary Care (Hospitals)	Stratifying the total throughput in Accident & Emergency and speed of admissions through focusing on bed turnover ratio in most congested Hospital Wards (as medical wards) and setting discharge and priority for beds based on Urgency of the cases.	Challenges and Quests

Mini-games within other activities (i.e. within the different departments)

Real-time feedback | Access and social feedback (1)

Mastery (4) |

'Behavioural Economics'

Type of Healthcare Services	Type of Gamification Activities Used in the Inspiration Labs Projects/ Models	Gamification Techniques	Constructs Indicators
	Codifying the Capacity of managing the availability of the Capacity of Beds Utilisation by inspiring towards higher discharges on time and based on defined protocols & follow-up services.	Levels Progress bars Trophy Case (Best Bed Management Wards)	Quantity and Time (4)
	Gauge the reduction of Antibiotics uses in the main referral hospital.	Challenges and Quests	Reputation (3)
	Gauge the 'Peers Review Practice' for Complex Cases.	Real-time Feedback	Quantity and time (3)
	Gauging the capacity of having the essential drug's availability in the main pharmacy, year-round.	Challenges and Quests	
28. Public Health Services	Codifying the 'Intelligent Inspection' that minimise the rate of poisonous calls, or low hygiene fines by 90% with less manpower and more trustworthiness enhancement.	Avatars (the idea of Training instead of Inspecting) Trophy case (Best Training)	Visual Cues (1) Reputation (3)
	Codify the reputation of fast food services that supports local tourism.	Achievements / badges	

Type of Healthcare Services	Type of Gamification Activities Used in the Inspiration Labs Projects/ Models	Gamification Techniques	Constructs Indicators
	Codify level of intelligence of the inspection based on the outcome of hospitality services and with minimal resources.	Levels Leaderboards Progress bars	Performance (3)
29. Health Enrichment	Codify the 'Quality of Life' practices & style in coordination with Health Centres	Achievements / badges	Reward Scheduling (1)
30. Psychiatric Services	Gauge the capacity to manage the anxiety to avoid reaching the level of chronic anxiety. Gauge suicide ratio due to early treatment of main causalities among youth. Gauge the patients' sick leave due to self-assessments of psycho-sematic symptoms	Real-time feedback (Through Self-Assessment Anxiety Forms) Challenges and quests Activity Feeds	Visual storytelling (1) Performance (3) Quantity and time (3)

Based on the analysis of the primary five constructs we can find 7 of the 21 activities (33%) to be of mechanical reference, 2 activities (10%) to be rewards reference, 9 activities (43%) to be of measurement reference and finally 3 activities (14%) to be of behaviour reference where the percentages are illustrated in Figure (2).

'Behavioural Economics'

Figure (2) Type of Constructs used in the Re-Invented Public Healthcare Projects

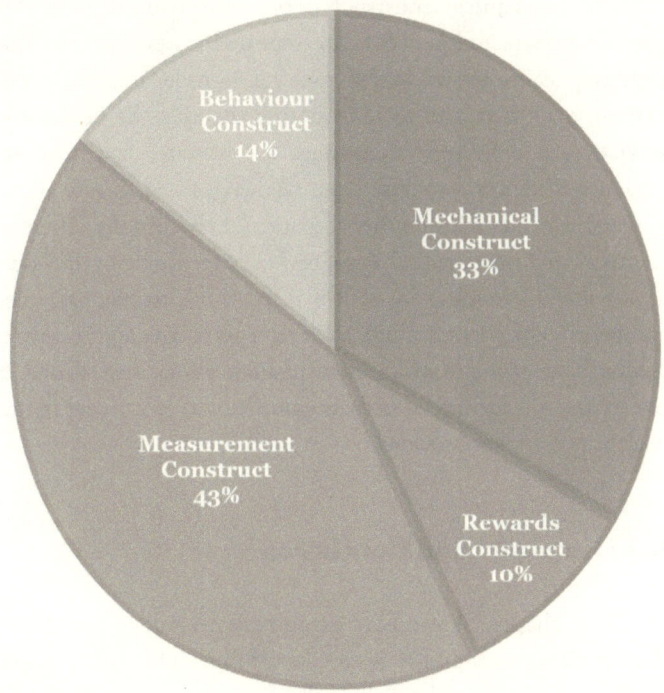

8.5 Findings

Majority of public healthcare services shows to be focused on measurement constructs, followed by mechanical constructs. In this chapter, we shall focus mainly on the findings of the measurement and the mechanical constructs as they carry 76% of the total activities done in relevant to labs efforts taken.

The measurement constructs used in the inspiration labs that led to re-inventing the healthcare services, came as a result of the following gamification techniques in relevance to the different activities developed: leader-boards, levels, interactions, establishing avatars, activity feeds, challenges and quests, achievements badges, leaderboards and progress bars.

The mechanical construct is the collective effort of the gamification techniques that are repeatedly were used in the different healthcare services sectors. I.e. in order to achieve the desired goals that lead to re-inventing the way the healthcare services are delivered, techniques as: hit-rate, codification, response alertness, progress bars, challenges and quests along with mini-games within other activities (i.e. within the different departments) were applied. Also, real-time feedback, avatars (i.e. as the idea of training instead of inspecting), trophy case (i.e. competition for best training), achievements badges and real-time feedback, i.e. through self-assessment anxiety forms; were used as part of the mechanical constructs gamification techniques in the healthcare services provided.

8.6 Discussion and Conclusion

This chapter shows how gamification could differentiate the health services and re-invent its efficacy. The gamification used in inspiration labs during the four years' projects in the Kingdom of Bahrain shows that there could be many innovative possibilities for healthcare improvement through the techniques and constructs of gamification.

The indirect rewards built as part of the labs and projects approaches helped to align the stakeholders of the different service, i.e. the medical and healthcare staff. This helped to overcome the challenges of change that usually are faced with professional bureaucratic that are usually available in healthcare organisation and cultures. The different gamification techniques helped avoid the mixed signals about the focus of change and improved the possibility of finding opportunities inside each of the problems in the inspiration labs.

The gamification constructs help to make almost all the interventions psychologically acceptable. The mechanical and measurement constructs gamified 76% of the healthcare services. Rewards construct constitute 10% of the gamified healthcare services and helped to balance their speed and accuracy, as in improving the quality of inspiring families' physicians and codifying patients self-triage, according to their level of emergency in health-centres while the behavioural construct constituted 14% of the total inspiration labs carried in the different healthcare sectors and was limited to the enhancement of both the social workers and the health visitors in the families screening.

Collectively, all the four constructs helped to effectively gamify the performance of the inspiration lab in re-inventing the healthcare services towards the benefits of early detection of disease, or speeding up the throughput of services, or mitigation of health risks, or improving the accessibility of emergency cases. This means that due to the nature of healthcare, many services can be gamified to the benefits of the patients' safety and quality of life.

The limitations of this study are that it is being carried in one country and as part of government inspiration labs. However, the study does not undermine recommending future studies that would explore further the influence of each gamification construct or indicators on the public healthcare services or similar other critical public services as education, municipality services, transportation, electricity and water supply and even security services. Development of interaction between all the stakeholders of these public services through the gamification techniques could help to further re-invent all these quality of life-related services to the benefit of citizens and the country in general.

References

Buheji, M (2019a) 'The Trust Project' Building better accessibility to Healthcare Services through BE and Inspiration Labs, International Journal of Economics, Commerce and Management, United Kingdom, Vol. VII, Issue 2, February.

Buheji, M (2019b) Shaping the Anatomy of Socio-Economic Community Problems towards Effective Solutions, Issues in Social Science, Vol. 7, No. 1, pp. 1-11.

Buheji, M. (2018) Re-Inventing Our Lives, A Handbook for Socio-Economic "Problem-Solving", AuthorHouse, UK.

Buheji, M and Ahmed, D (2018) Exploring Inspiration Economy, AuthorHouse, UK.

Buheji, M and Ahmed, D (2017) Breaking the Shield- Introduction to Inspiration Engineering: Philosophy, Practices and Success Stories, Archway Publishing, FROM SIMON & SCHUSTER, USA.

Buhijji, A (2017) The 9 Characters of Creativity, the development of a creativity tool-kit for idea generation in collaborative design projects. Master in Innovation Design Thesis, Brunel University, UK.

Deci, E., Ryan, R. (1985) Intrinsic motivation and self-determination in human behavior, Plenum Press, New York.

Deterding, S., S., Khaled, R., Nacke, L., Dixon, D. (2013) Gamification: Toward a Definition, Proceedings of the CHI 2011, Vancouver, Interaction Design and Architecture(s) Journal - IxD&A, N.19, pp. 28-37 9.

Deterding, S., Khaled, R., Nacke, L., Dixon, D. (2011) From Game Design Elements to Gamefulness: Defining "Gamification", Proceedings of the MindTrek 2011, Tampere.

Domínguez, A., Saenz-de-Navarrete, J., de-Marcos, L., Fernández-Sanz, L., Pagés, C., Martínez-Herráiz, J. (2013)

Gamifying learning experiences: Practical implications and outcomes, Computers & Education, 63, pp. 380--392

Hense, J. and Mandl, H (2012) Learning in or with games? Quality criteria for digital learning games from the perspectives of learning, emotion, and motivation theory, In: D.G. Sampson, J. M. Spector, D. Ifenthaler & P. Isaias (eds.), Proceedings of the IADIS International Conference on Cognition and Exploratory Learning in the Digital Age, pp. 19-26, IADIS,

Heckhausen, J., Heckhausen, H. (2008) Motivation and action: Cambridge University Press, Cambridge.

Kapp, K (2012) The Gamification of Learning and Instruction: Game-based Methods and Strategies for Training and Education, Pfeiffer, San Francisco.

Madrid, W and Hunter, D (2012) For the Win: How Game Thinking Can Revolutionize Your Business., Wharton Digital Press, Philadelphia.

McClelland, D.C. (2009) Human motivation, Cambridge University Press, Cambridge.

McGonigal, J. (2011) Reality Is Broken: Why Games Make Us Better and How They Can Change the World, Penguin Group, New York

Robinson, D. and Bellotti, V. (2013) A Preliminary Taxonomy of Gamification Elements for Varying Anticipated Commitment, Proceedings of the CHI, Paris.

Rughiniș, R. (2013) Flexible Gamification in a Social Learning Situation. Insights from a Collaborative Review Exercise, Proceedings of the CSCL 2013, Munich.

Ryan, R. and Deci, E. (2000) Self-determination theory and the facilitation of intrinsic motivation, social development, and well-being, American psychologist, 55(1), pp. 68—78.

Sailer, M; Hense, J, Mandl, H and Klevers, M (2013) Psychological Perspectives on Motivation through Gamification,

Interaction Design and Architecture(s) Journal - IxD&A, N.19, 2013, pp. 28-37.

Skinner, B. (1963) Operant Behavior, American Psychologist, 18(8), pp. 503—515. 18.

Werbach, K., & Hunter, D. (2012) For the Win: How Game Thinking Can Revolutionize Your Business. Philadelphia: Wharton Digital Press.

CONCLUSION

Behavioural economics and its related economies, as inspiration economy, focus in creating positive transformation in the public practices and policies through capitalising on hidden or lost opportunities. BE and IE work on changing the behaviour or the mindset of the stakeholders to create the targeted change through initiatives sometimes called Nudge or Inspiration Labs.

All the problems solved by both BE and IE start first by diagnosing how the people of the community think. Then how this thinking can be guided or facilitated towards the betterment of the targeted community. Based on this basic thinking there are lots of QoL initiatives that have been brought by both BE and IE, that is beyond the scope of this book, which can be referred too.

The overlook of the theme of the messages of this book illustrates that both BE and IE help to build bridges for excessive confidence and make the stakeholders feel the ownership of the change that needs to be created. Also, both BE and IE bring in diverse solutions relevant to QoL in areas as healthcare, education, corruption, poverty and unemployment.

The editors show from the assessment of the recent developments in the behavioural economics (BE) and the socio-economic literature that there is still a gap in the body of knowledge, between the methodologies, or the tools of BE and similar techniques in one side the targeted impact. In this book, we present the purpose of any methodology of BE, IE and gamification in creating a differentiation in the quality of life. Despite that BE, IE and gamification can be described as methodologies of creating immediate change, the targeted condition or environment, these methodologies could also play a significant role in setting future foresight that eliminates coming challenges and improve the policies relevance to different sectors.

The blending of both BE with the benefit of IE methodologies in this book is meant to enhance the effect of 'architecting of choices' which perfectly synchronise with the contemporary and foresighted challenges of QoL. The developed formula BE + IE + Stakeholders Engagement found to bring us faster to QoL practices which their absence has been chronic for a long time.

One of the main outcomes of this work is that it sets a better awareness about new radical approaches that could be used for eliminating the widening communities' disparities which could be seen clearly in the rising levels of the different life inequalities today. The reader hopefully would see that BE started to lead the new economic influence in shaping the QoL in ways never experienced before. The other two coming socio-economic driven concepts: Inspiration Economy and Gamification are also planning a new profound role in shaping further different QoL issues that have been chronic for long time. Therefore, we propose the following framework for QoL concerned researchers, planners and decision-makers, as shown in Figure (0-1). The proposed framework not only shows the influence caused by BE, IE and Gamification on the contemporary QoL, but also in its role in raising the capacity for more accurate 'Future Foresight'.

Figure (0-1) Illustrate the Influence that could be made on QoL from BE, Inspiration Economy and Gamification.

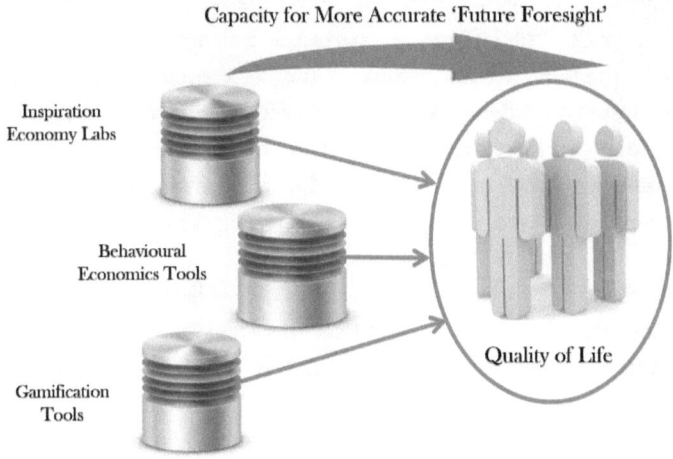

As editors of this book, we have tried to show the relation of both BE and IE, utilising the empathetic mindset and their impact on both hedonic and eudemonic well-being. Therefore, the chapters did not carry lots of technical data about classical economic indicators like GDP, wellbeing, happiness and quality of life. Nevertheless, the cases discussed in the different chapters triggers the visualisation of the reader about the BE impact on any or all of these economic QoL indicators; if the empirically tested models are generalised.

It can be noted also that the outline of this work avoided the traditional economic books approach, i.e. history of the BE as a concept and its relation to QoL' or how they both should be measured, is intentionally avoided. The intent was here to build a holistic perspective for the reader and excite him to participate in creating positive change, while appreciating the economic, the sociological and psychological input.

This edited book brought new ways of thinking by linking how BE and its related IE could shape our QoL. The first part focuses on BE Influence on QoL. Here the first chapter discusses the new BE influence using the Nudge and inspiration labs literature which were applied by the researcher for the last five years. The chapter compares the different BE approaches and their impact on 'quality of life' as a potential source for communities' development. The chapter reflects lots of case studies conducted and published by the researcher in different countries, which helped to realise the importance of QoL focused problems solving, specifically in developing countries.

The second chapter, reviews the architecting of the QoL in relevance to emergency patients. The blended BE and IE approaches bring in first a codification system in five participating health centres. The piloted projects were monitored on how they influenced patients' behaviour and thus help in the elimination of their risk of collapse, before being diagnosed in the right time. The psychology of trust using nudge and inspiration economies labs are discussed in relevance to their effective mechanism in creating positive change to all the stakeholders. Finally, the researcher recommends more fieldwork to be continued in this line to ease the life and the needs of the community.

Chapter three, concludes with further recommendations of utilising the choices and the variety of approaches that both Nudge and Inspiration Labs brings to different governmental and societal QoL issues. Keeping government BE projects open-minded to beyond Nudge techniques is one the conclusion of this chapter. Creating new cultures attitudes is found to be highly related to any community variety of solutions.

Chapter four, and through its qualitative research, helped to provide a theoretical framework for gamification approaches in the different sectors of the public services through enhancing the engagement of the stakeholders of these services. The findings show the opportunities for the government transformation that could come from gamifying essential QoL sectors like education, water utility services, labour management, women affairs, traffic management, sewage and sanitary service, social insurance, police services and justice and legal affairs. The study concludes with recommendations for further empirical studies that would enhance the integration of gamification approaches in re-inventing the public services and specifically QoL.

The second part of the book is about QoL influences on the future foresighted socio-economic life. The part starts with the fifth chapter that discusses the differentiated results of the two concepts of behavioural economic pros and cons and how researchers and practitioners can benefit from their lesson learned and clear achievements. The chapter shows the importance of multidisciplinary applications that lead to the improvement of communities' QoL and in how this linked to the way the human mindset is utilised.

Chapter six, take us into a journey in future for the critical areas of BE, such as the bounded rationality, the psychological economics, the behavioural finance, besides the nudging and the behavioural macroeconomics. The chapter reviews where the BE contributions today and where it might go in the future. Recommendation for further research is suggested about how to optimise BE for future demand.

Chapter seven, focuses on raising the future detection capacity of the reader and the stakeholders through understanding what to mitigate QoL risks as the rise of NCD's Risks through Foresight economy lab (FEL). The researchers show how to drastically reduce the percentage of the at NCD's population and avoid the plague risk in the future.

Chapter eight, exploits the findings presented around the opportunities and the learning that comes from gamifying the change initiatives. The chapter shows how researchers and practitioners can gamify complex public services, as healthcare sectors, and create a change to different activities that would lead to a behavioural change of the targeted community. The study makes a recommendation to considers more in-depth empirical studies that enhance the integration of gamification in more public services.

We hope that this book managed to convince you as a reader and research that by giving more focus on BE, IE techniques, and gamification techniques we could improve the aspired QoL standards and create more future sustainable results with best optimisation of resources.

ABBREVIATIONS

Behavioural Economics (BE)
Foresight Economy Lab (FEL)
IE Labs (IL's)
Inspiration Economy (IE)
Non-Communicable Disease (NCDs)
Quality of Life (QoL)

KEYWORDS

Behavioral Economics, Inspiration Economy, Inspiration Economy Labs, Gamification, Quality of Life, Future Foresight, Socio-Economic Issues.

WHO WE ARE

The *International Inspiration Economy Project (IIEP)* is a collection of focused efforts that target to advance and spread the concepts, the development tools, through series of socio-economic problems solving projects, supported by way of forums, labs, academic programs, publications and workshops delivery. IIEP uses different means to spread its message through its own international institutions, collaborating NGO's societies, peer-reviewed journals, books and global partners'. Under the IIEP, there are four main concepts: **Inspiration Economy (IE), Resilience Economy (RE) and Youth Economy (YE), which all use Foresight Economy (FE).** All of these four economy based approaches work together towards solving chronic socio-economic issues with minimal resources and based on the concept of **"Influencing without Power".** They target to show the possibilities models that bring the outcome to the world and create a legacy by using **the intrinsic human powers.**

Contact us

Dr Mohamed Buheji & Dr Dunya Ahmed

Founder - International Institute of Inspiration Economy
www.inspirationeconomy.org

Founder - Youth Economy Forums
www.youtheconomy.org

Founding Editor - International Journal of Youth Economy (Published in 1st May & 1st Nov.)
http://naturalspublishing.com/show.asp?JorID=56&pgid=0

Founding Editor - International Journal of Inspiration & Resilience Economy (Published in 1st March & 1st Sep.)
http://www.sapub.org/journal/aimsandscope.aspx?journalid=1145

BRIEF ABOUT EDITORS

Dr Mohamed Buheji is the founders of the International Institute of Inspirational Economy and *considered a leading expert in the areas of **Excellence, Knowledge, Innovation, Inspiration, Change Management** and **enhancement of Competitiveness** for over 25 years. He is a retired professor from the University of Bahrain. Besides being **a Future Foresighter. He** is also the **Founder of the International Journal of Inspiration & Resilience Economy and International Journal of Youth Economy.** He has published since 2008 more than 70 peer-reviewed journal and conference papers and 17 books in the subject of the **power of thinking, lifelong learning, quality of life, inspiration and competitiveness.** Also, he has **five books in English about Knowledge-Economy, Inspiration Economy, Inspiring Government and Inspiration Engineering, Resilience Economy and Youth Economy.** He is passionate about transferring his + 500 consultancy projects experience for more than 300 organisations from all over the world, to both education and research. Besides, he serves in the editorial board of 5 internationally peer-reviewed journals. He is a member of many scientific communities, journals, academic review boards. Lately, he is a winner of many awards including the latest **CEEMAN best researcher award for 2017**, besides being a **Fellow of World Academy of Productivity Science.***

Address: International Institute of Inspirational Economy, P.O.Box 37313, Bahrain [e-mail: buhejim@gmail.com, web site: www.buheji.com]

Dr Dunya Ahmed Abdulla Ahmed is an **assistant professor** and lecturer in the Department of Social Sciences at the University of Bahrain & **Strategic Planning & Development Adviser** in Supreme Council for Women. In addition, she is **Scientific Committee Chairperson in Institute of Inspiration Economy, EU & MENA.** She completed her PhD at the University of Warwick, to be the first and only person hold a PhD in social work in Bahrain, specialized and concentrates mainly on gender equity and the rights of people with disabilities. She is **co-founder of Inspiration Economy concept, Journals, projects & institutions around the world.** She is also Editorial Board of several international scientific journals. In addition to being an active member of several NGOs & **president of Inspiration Economy Society** in Bahrain. She has also contributed to the preparation and implementation of a number of national strategies, and preparation and discussion of international reports.

Address: Department of Social Sciences, College of Art, University of Bahrain, P.O. Box 32038, Kingdom of Bahrain and Inspiration Economy Society, Kingdom of Bahrain. [e-mail: dr.dunya@hotmail.com]

www.ingramcontent.com/pod-product-compliance
Lightning Source LLC
Chambersburg PA
CBHW020645220526
45464CB00001B/302